# FALLING TOGETHER

*A family's story of mental illness and grief*

## DONNA McCART SHARKEY

**DEMETER**

**Falling together**
A family's story of mental illness and grief
Donna McCart Sharkey

Demeter Press
2546 10th Line
Bradford, Ontario
Canada, L3Z 3L3
Tel: 289-383-0134
Email: info@demeterpress.org
Website: www.demeterpress.org

Demeter Press logo based on the sculpture "Demeter" by Maria-Luise Bodirsky www.keramik-atelier.bodirsky.de

Printed and Bound in Canada

Cover artwork: *Power to the Favela*, a clay and encaustic painting by Diana Smith, from the series *Abstract the News*
Cover layout and typesetting: Michelle Pirovich

Library and Archives Canada Cataloguing in Publication
Title: Falling together: a family's story of mental illness and grief / Donna McCart Sharkey.
Names: Sharkey, Donna, author.
Identifiers: Canadiana 20200374982 | ISBN 9781772583502 (softcover)
Subjects: LCSH: Sharkey, Donna. | LCSH: Sharkey, Donna—Family. | LCSH: Parental grief. | LCSH: Loss (Psychology) | LCSH: Families of the mentally ill. | LCSH: Parents of mentally ill children—Biography. | LCSH: Motherhood—Psychological aspects. | LCGFT: Autobiographies.
Classification: LCC BF575.G7 S53 2021 | DDC 152.4—dc23

For my daughter, Renata,
a woman of courage and brilliance

*The ache for home lives in all of us, the safe place where we can go as we are and not be questioned.*

—Maya Angelou


*Persons appear to us according to the light we throw upon them from our own minds.*

—Laura Ingalls Wilder

# Contents

# Prologue

I looked up and saw a sign on a country store that read: *You don't have to be depressed just because you're here.* That was a dream, and it was four years after. I wasn't certain I was ready to leave my sadness then. I wasn't sure I had anything to replace it.

The weight of familiar shame and embarrassment—there, like a thick coat I find myself wearing—requires undoing. How strong the desire to pass, for my family to pass as typical, just like everyone else. How strong the hope we won't get caught out. How strong, too, the disseverment, locked out from much that used to function as a source of succor. This was my world.

The leaning away from chaos with its particular toll.

Like many, I have been formed as a witness.

# PART I

Alessandra lived big. Even so, no one ever planned for this.


I'll tell

you about my daughter.


*It better be true,* she would say.


How else to go.

How to remember a life? From beginning to end or end to beginning? From fragments—flashes of brightness, sparkles, an object that brings a treasured moment to mind? From a tightness in your fingers, the strain of trying to hold onto hope.

Or panic in the darkest of the night, rumbles of fear, ground shaking underneath with the ring of the phone, a mention of a dank shelter, tumult, sadness echoing as in a chamber, anger—mostly held in check, but not always—crises piled over crises, loss then more loss piled over the last, then more loss.

If she had heard it from someone else, she would have thought, don't do that to yourself. Back away. Protect yourself. But she kept at it, the rest of her family more and more overshadowed. This is what she saw through the layers of memory as she knows them, her best unearthing.

And in the overhang, her failure to save her daughter.

# Home

## Finding

I had never been inside an orphanage, but tucked in the backseat of our family Studebaker on our way to visit our grandparents, even before we got to it, we sat fascinated in its spell: stone walls, enormous like a castle, maybe larger, the thrall of the lives of the children inside. Back in our bedroom, my sister and I taunted each other. "You're adopted. They're going to send you to an orphanage." "Not me," I said. "I won't go to an orphanage."

I'm thirty-three, my mother's age when I was born, and it's four weeks after her diagnosis of terminal illness when I start the process to adopt a child. I don't share this plan with my mother. It seems too cruel to discuss my life without her in it. How to tell her she may have a grandchild she will never meet?

When a social worker from the adoption agency calls me about a child, for reasons now obscure, I say no, not her. I carry guilt for two weeks for rejecting this child. When I'm told about Alessandra, I know she's my daughter and I say yes. Later, I'm also told that she has a sister, Renata, three years old, whom I will also adopt, although Alessandra and I will have to wait a year and a half before Renata's adoption is finalized and she comes to live with us.

The agency's report speaks of Alessandra as a restless eight-year-old girl, possibly hyperactive. I consult a specialist but hold onto the position that hyperactivity is merely more active, lively, energetic, surely positive traits, not the grim, prickly picture painted by a friend who claims to know. I think of my father, working in a mine in Scotland as a teen, and later, running a successful business in Canada, constantly moving, fidgeting, engaging anyone who would listen to him. Surely hyperactivity can't be all that bad.

But "hyperactivity" will be more than what I imagine, much more, although this thought doesn't cross my mind at the time.

In the picture I receive, she looks downcast, eyes sad yet resolute, a prominent scar above her right eye, her hair close to shaven. I put the picture on the mantle in my living room and when I walk into the room, I say, "Hi, Alessandra."

Several months later, with her picture tucked in my wallet, I sunnily fly to Brazil to bring my daughter home. The orphanage where she lives is not a fairy-tale castle. More like a worn convent. Walking up the lane toward its oversized wooden doors, I notice my stride slowing. In a few steps I will be inside and will meet Alessandra. I knock and a girl opens the door but turns away quickly. Is she my daughter?

Inside, the foyer holds dark furniture, oversized pictures of saints, popes, and Christ about to die, covered in blood, hanging desolately on his Cross. The orphanage director, Sister Madelena, greets me. I am the first foreigner to come there.

I tour the building and sign documents, then someone brings Alessandra into the director's office. Looking fearful, she is told to count to ten in English and she does this joylessly, staring at the floor. We're introduced. I smile. I say my practiced Portuguese greeting phrases and she whispers a reply, still staring at the floor. I'm assured the deep scars above her left eye and on her arms and legs are a result of play and it's only then that I realize the orphanage has few toys, no playground.

We leave the director's office and when someone brings Renata to me, I hold her in my arms while she eyes me seriously. As eighty girls sing a plaintive farewell song to Alessandra, I pick up my camera, hiding behind it as I fight back tears. After the song, children surround me, delicately touching my arms and hands, the older ones beseeching, "Please be my mother, too. Take me with you." But I'm not even able to take Renata with us.

Alessandra and I leave the orphanage. She wears a t-shirt, shorts, and flipflops—all her belongings. She dashes into our taxi, and as we drive away she doesn't glance back. I hold her passport tight, her picture inside it seared with sadness.

In the late afternoon in São Paulo, we eat our dinner quickly in our hotel room as I wonder how to spend this first evening with a stranger who speaks a different language from me. But she is happy to teach me Portuguese words and I'm happy to exchange these for the English equivalent.

The next morning I'm startled awake. Alessandra is standing at the edge of my bed staring down at me. How long has she been there, staring?

Orphanages can harm a child's development and health. As a child's brain develops, new synaptic connections which are formed through stimulation and experience support social and cognitive development. Orphanages can put children at risk of neglect, attention deficit disorder, difficulty forming healthy relationships, and mental illnesses. Workers come and go and children, already separated from birth parents, may also be separated from siblings. How to cope with this loss, how to understand life, be protected from harm, love oneself?

# Home

## First

A postwar suburb, edged from a city, and naïve to diversity. That's where I grew up. Which I did in a hollow sort of way, frightened of what Hell might hold for me, fearful of the A-bomb, and even more scared of authority. We were told that downtown was dangerous, filled with men who might grab us into white slavery. We heard stories of cockroaches in slums, mafiosi with guns. And yet, I held one thought deeply: *Get out when you can.*

On my first day of kindergarten, I have high hopes, and when I spy a wooden stick horse I run to it fast and ride it, circling the room until the teacher dashes towards me demanding I give it to a boy, a toy for boys, not girls. How shamed I felt, for her scolding. How shamed I felt for not knowing.

That same year my mother sews pink bedspreads with pleated skirts and flowered pillow covers and curtains for my sister and me. My Barbara Ann Scott doll sits on my pillow; my sister's walking doll sits on hers. I'm not sure why I'm often angry in that room, but one day, seething for a reason I no longer recall, I cut three large slices out of my bedspread's skirt with my mother's shearing scissors. Moments later, remorseful, I confess to her. Holding me tight as she rocks the anger out of me, she tells me she doesn't want me to grow up to be like my father, with his short temper. Nor do I, and after that day the sharp of my expressed anger softens.

Six months later, my sister and I undergo surgery to correct gaps in our front teeth, considered unattractive. Our father had separations between his teeth, visible in pictures of him until he was thirty, when his teeth were replaced with dentures. My parents never expected perfect daughters, but they do want passable girls—girls who won't embarrass them or shame them with imperfect gaps between their teeth. Girls who keep the veneer of suburban niceness.

The gap corrected, my anger pushed down, I stand out less in a group and no longer speak too loudly. I read books, play classical music on the piano, and try hard at school. I fear authority figures and become reticent, cautious in public, hoping to fit in.

Which also means:

I embarrass easily and blush red too often as shame continues to run, fulsome, through my girlhood

in which, embroiled in our family religious battles, my sister and I are transferred to a Catholic school when I am in grade two, she in grade four,

where we wear white: shoes with a slim strap, gloves with a frill at the wrist and an exquisitely delicate button, a mini-size wedding-like dress, a veil held by a plastic headband, a pearlized prayer book with a thin cord—our First Communion. We are older than the others, all in grade one, and already easy with their taunts when they sense difference. We are the Protestants-turned-Catholics who, in our futures, will turn elsewhere, but for now aren't able to recite the prayers, don't know the answer to the first question of the Catechism, who made you, why, are last to file into the Presentation-de-la-Sainte-Vierge and last to receive communion.

Shortly after, my communion clothes disappear from the house. Then the other Catholic items: a holy card, a tiny statue of Anthony—patron saint of lost items—my pale blue rosary beads with a delicate silver cross. I know not to ask about the missing items. Again, I feel shame, but don't know why.

Even now, many years later, there are times when I'm not sure why I feel shame.

# Home

## New

In the beginning, after Alessandra arrived, we were the picture of a modern family—until the image shifted and mental illness became its fulcrum, the family's centrepiece.

The first week, we drive by a used car dealership, its lot festooned with balloons advertising a sale. Alessandra shrieks excitedly, "Fiesta!" As I laugh with her, her exuberance and joy in living seem like they will last forever.

Each afternoon at the living room window I watch her skip home from her school down the street. She's happy, but boisterous in class, out of her seat too often. Within weeks, her teacher requests a meeting. Attention Deficit Hyperactivity Disorder, ADHD, enters as the first of the labels that Alessandra will gather over time. Medication becomes part of her daily routine, and her teacher breathes a sigh of relief. The medication lasts until 6:00 p.m. when curiosity, cool focus, and sustained concentration overturn to bustling commotion. Each evening, I hold on.

I leave the city to attend a work conference and two of my friends stay overnight with my daughter. When I come home the following day, they ask me, "How do you do it?" One says, "We're exhausted, we hardly slept, and when we came downstairs to the kitchen in the morning, we found that we had left the back door open, no, not unlocked, wide open."

How I want Alessandra to fit in. How intensely I want her to be a passable girl. I enroll her in a swimming class with four other girls, two years younger and all friends with each other. How thoughtfully she picks her turquoise and pink flowered bathing suit. But after that first class, after one girl tells her that her bathing suit is ugly, she won't return.

When her school year ends, we visit Saturna Island, where each day at the beach she explores the shoreline. Returning to the cottage at day's end, sun soaked, we walk along a dirt road as Alessandra's medication swishes out of her body like a waterfall and she runs, cartwheels, and handstands her way home where, for her, a sit-down dinner is a near impossibility.

Then early one evening, something unexpected happens at the cottage. Like a great egret who can stand for extended periods of time, its body still, anticipating, Alessandra stays steady. Close to a bird feeder, waiting for a nearby hummingbird to land on her finger, knowing it will, her right arm is outstretched, her index finger fixed to accept the bird's landing. Abruptly, the bird is in front of her, hovering, staring at her. The rest of us in nearby canvas chairs, scarcely breathing, will it to land. The bird darts forward and grasps Alessandra's finger. They look at each other, both focusing intently, until the hummingbird flies backward, then is gone.

She's my rock and roll dance partner and we love to jive. Dancing holds us together, keeps us in rhythm with each other, in the moment. To imaginary audiences, we perform "Girls Just Want to Have Fun," not caring if we don't get the words right. "Always on My Mind," "Heartbeat," "Are You Lonesome Tonight?" "That'll Be the Day."

Alessandra is ready for each adventure—a road trip, a hike in the woods, a swim in a lake. I'm the events coordinator, her trusted person, who can, at times just passably, at other times more effectively, calm her when the waves of her inner sea become too rough. I'm her guide— somewhat—through her sorrows. Sometimes her cheerleader, other times her rock.

During the next year, we have enormous fun. Mostly. I begin to see more cracks in her exuberance and joy of living. She tells me of being punished and left overnight in the orphanage basement with its dirt floor, no bed, no washroom, no lights, too many bats. She plays with a porcelain doll, and throwing it onto the floor of a closet and slamming the door, she commands: "You'll stay in there all night, you're bad, I'll hurt you."

Millions of people were affected by the 1998 ice storm in eastern Canada and the United States. In some places, widespread power outages lasted over a month. To determine how hardship during pregnancy affects a child's well-being, health, and cognitive development, Project Ice Storm followed 150 children whose mothers were pregnant during that storm. Genetic changes in the DNA of these children were found and the study concluded these children may be at heightened risk of developing behaviour problems, autism, asthma, type 2 diabetes, or obesity.

# Home

## Full

At times, we fear that Renata will never join our family. Since Alessandra's adoption, regulations have changed, leading to a process with new complexities.

Unable to protect her sister, Alessandra often feels frantic about the wait. By the time her adoption is finally approved, the toddler I met in Brazil is now four years old. Sharing the same birth mother, they now also share me.

Renata flies from Brazil to New York with a representative from the adoption agency, and I'm there waiting at the airport to bring her home. Her plane has arrived and still they don't appear. I pace until I hear my name called over a loudspeaker and I race to see Renata propped on a tall counter beside an immigration agent. I produce documents, then I hold her in my arms, and she curls into my body. I breathe easy. Home soon.

Arriving at our home airport, friends and Alessandra cheer as the doors swing open and movie star-like, we sweep through the rooms. Relief. Really home. Renata slips easily into family life. School, though, is different. She joins a class with mostly English language learners, but over three months my apprehension grows as she speaks no English. Alessandra had daily scaffolded language learning, so Renata's style baffles me. Until one day she communicates in full sentences.

Alessandra belongs to a small class for children designated as having special needs—code for children who, among other issues, abhor sitting still, even for short periods of time. I measure a day successful when her teacher doesn't phone concerning a behavior issue; an evening successful if her take-home note exclaims, *Bravo!*

In my school, where rote learning and group repetition were the norm, the teachers, almost all nuns, assumed obedience. We bowed to a nun when she passed in the hall. We curtsied when the school principal entered our classroom, and we greeted her in unison. Good morning, Sister Zita. At our seats, we stayed with fingers laced, palms compliant on the edge of our desks. We learned to confess sins to priests. Special needs classes were unheard-of.

Now, meetings to determine next steps, testing by a school psychologist, a teacher expecting me to be part of a team, all this unfamiliar territory. I read, research, talk to experts, begin to grow nervous for Alessandra's future.

Searching for an explanation, I surmise that issues during pregnancy may be an influencing factor.


Even a mother's stress can alter a fetus's brain development. These changes may be long-lasting or permanent.


Evenings, Alessandra and I read together; though by now, free from medication, tender poems turn into raucous thrills. "Alligator Pie," "Tony Baloney," and "Billy Batter" bounce off her bed and ricochet wildly from one wall to another. They squeal and jam and along the way, "Mumbo Jumbo" squeezes its way into the gang, the cacophony loudly signaling resistance to sleep. As though lit by psychedelic disco lights, the room seems to swirl to a blaring beat. Like Ecstasy. For Alessandra, not for me.Tired after long days at work, ecstasy for me would be a soft pillow.

Hoping this will not be a nuit blanche for my daughter, I bless her with stardust gently flicked from the tips of my fingers. "This will put you to sleep," I say, leaving her room, slumping to mine like someone in a drowsed opium-induced stupor. Although I'll likely be woken several times during the night, I hope I'll make it through the next workday.

A friend calls later in the evening. "Hi, how are you? What's new?"

Earlier in the evenings, I read with Renata and we make up stories, serial adventures that continue for weeks. Tucked into me, she wants stories of small girls stuck in dangerous situations then emerging victorious, the world proving itself a safe place. She supplies the names for the girls, her name and Fiona, her best friend's name. She pushes for details until, wrapped in the story, she slides into sleep.

Older, she reads *The Lion, the Witch and the Wardrobe, Matilda, and Carrie's War.* Older still, the Holocaust holds her world, a world of danger, at times with luck, escape. Even older, serial killers and mass murderers.

I note differences between Alessandra and Renata, their language learning styles, their distinct ways of processing trauma and loss. What might this mean for the future? And because they are girls who are Black, how will their futures be affected?

# Home

## Still passing

I try to soften the effects of ADHD and a learning disability on Alessandra's social, emotional, and educational life, and although she continues to suffer, we continue to manage.

Adrenalin-fueled activities and risk-taking attract her. Fearless, she dives from the highest diving boards and climbs to the uppermost branches of trees. She wants to be a fire fighter or join a police force. I'm thrilled, and in my mind I see her searching for a lost child, working as a dog handler, saving lives. She is athletic, kind, an extrovert, and oriented toward social justice and the best in others. She would excel at either choice. But she will do neither of these.

Trauma changes the very nature of the brain. A traumatized brain needs repair.

Adverse childhood experiences (ACEs) are traumatic experiences that negatively affect a child's development and long-term success. ACEs can lead to anxiety disorder, PTSD and disassociation, physical ailments, child development issues, relationship difficulties, and disordered sleep. They may also lower serotonin levels and lead to depression, heart disease, cancer, stroke, and increase the probability of suicide. Complex trauma held within a person's DNA is passed onto future generations.

Most of the staff at the after-school programmes are high school students. There is no training for this job, and typically, it's their first. I bring them donuts and chocolate and each afternoon on my way to pick up my daughters, I steel myself for the director. Often enough,

*Alessandra is too rambunctious.* I beg Alessandra to act calm. As a working mother, I need her to retain this space. After-school options are slim, and there is little tolerance for a girl with ADHD. They might keep her a month, sometimes longer, until the director has a sombre conversation with me. Each child needs attention, they don't have enough staff, they are drained by my daughter's uber-enthusiasm. *You will have to find a different programme.*

Alessandra continues to play fast, at the edge of risk. Falling off a swing at an after-school programme, she dislocates her elbow. The director brings her to emergency, her first hospital visit. Eventually, she will see the inside of five hospital emergency wards, will visit each one several times, and I will learn how to make my way around these places. But not without stress.

# Home

## Chaos

The universe is alive, and has fire in it, and is full of gods.

—Thales of Miletus

According to Hesiod, primal chaos was matter without form, infinite space, the foundation of reality, origin of all the gods, of the cosmos. Primal chaos existed before planets and stars, before our universe. Before we and our world existed.

When the chaos in our home began, it didn't take long for it to assemble, and I was unprepared.

Mayhem, upheaval, shambles, disarray, turmoil. For me, anyway, that's how it was becoming.

Alessandra turns nine. At home, her moods swing. She can't sleep, feels hopeless, and rails against herself. She shows me her big toe. I gasp—no nail. She has worked it off. Pulled it out completely.

When she turns ten, more unravels. She gives me a small note. *Mum, I want to die.* One morning, she is under her desk at school and incoherent. When I arrive at the children's hospital, where Alessandra and her teacher are waiting for me, I watch her, confused. Someone hands me a prescription for her and we leave. Driving home, I stop for ice cream. *Maybe this will make her feel better, make everything fine, make her coherent.* But of course not. What was I thinking?

Alessandra's eleven. Each morning, she takes medication and if she forgets, her teacher calls me by 9:00 a.m. She also calls for other reasons—my daughter's listening skills, attention, behaviour, are not up to par. Her friendships disrupt. She is often by herself at recess. Alessandra cuts her arms, her legs. She worries the cuts. They bleed in class.

When she's twelve, too many voices cram her head. School becomes more chaotic, and her teacher worries because concentration eludes her and she doesn't always follow guidelines. Alessandra aims toward life, joy, and sweetness, yet restless and distracted, she still has trouble keeping friends.

I ask myself the question, can love reverse this?

More razor marks line her arms. I take her to a psychiatrist who tells me that her adoption will break down before she turns thirteen. I bristle. *That will never happen.* He prescribes more and different psychiatric medications. She tries them, and re-adjusts. This cycle continues. In fact, it never stops. Nor do the effects of abandonment and—as I come to learn over time—the physical and sexual abuse she suffered before her adoption.

Alessandra doesn't want to be a teenager. When her teacher calls on a Thursday afternoon in October, for the second time I meet them at a hospital.

In the emergency waiting area Alessandra sits unmoving, scarily quiet. She doesn't look up when I speak to her. I hold her hand, but she doesn't appear to notice. She is unresponsive to the psychiatrist's questions, and what she does say is unclear. The psychiatrist looks over to me. "She needs to be admitted." I'm shocked. He talks on, I don't follow what he's saying. I'm still at *needs to be admitted.* My daughter, twelve, in a psychiatric ward. Where she will live for six months, where she will become a teenager.

The next morning, meeting with the ward psychiatrist, I watch my daughter, usually so strong and athletic, now unsteady. A nurse helps her down the hall. Once inside the psychiatrist's office, she crumples to the floor. I hear the term "psychotic episode." I stare at her, vulnerable, unmoving on the tile.

"She's too young," I say through tears. I ask for explanation. "Why? What does it mean? How long will it last?" But nothing is definite, and no one hands me any hope. I help my daughter up and walk her, lurching, back to her bed, where I cover her with a blanket. As I tuck it in close to her, something inside me shatters. I whisper to her, "This will pass." But she's somewhere else.

As I leave the hospital, I tell myself this is the worst that will happen to her. Perhaps she is purging past loss and harm from her psyche. The idea buoys me, although apart from my family, I don't speak to anyone about what happened. Too terrible to see my child in this situation, too much to grasp, too hard to express my feelings, to tell. And even though I trust that this will be short-lived, I fear people's judgment, of her, of me, of my family. I know it's pathetic to refuse to take the risk to be seen as pathetic, but I learned growing up to keep family secrets so that others would not think less of us. The last thing I want is for people to pity or dismiss my family, to view me as weak or incapable, unable to handle life's demands.

When Alessandra turns thirteen, I hire a clown to deliver balloons and treats to her hospital room. I pretend jolliness as Renata, Alessandra, and I eat pizza and cake, but I feel sluggish. Afterwards, Renata asks when her sister can come home. She misses her and I tell her I do too, but I don't tell her that I'm scared.

I long for Alessandra to recover and I form a belief that if I visit every day, my love, my presence, the strength of my will for her to get better will sway her in the direction of health. Renata often comes with me and never balks. Just as I feel sorry for Alessandra, I feel sorry for Renata. Our *how life is.*

Renata's *how life is* had never been ordinary. At two years old, she was left with her younger brother on a street in São Paulo. They were brought to a police station and from there sent to separate orphanages. At three, she was transferred to the orphanage where Alessandra was living and two months after that, Alessandra left to come to Canada. It took a year and a half for Renata to do the same, and by that time, her losses had piled so high: birth parents, brother, sister, language, all she knew. And now this. Another *how life is.*

I want to hold Renata in a protective cocoon to give her something approaching a regular childhood. But each crisis to come will follow its own storm path. Each tornado will touch down on the family. And while sometimes I can and do protect her, other times I'm unable to shield her from the vortex.

It's six months before Alessandra's psychotic break finally releases its grip and she comes home. I'm exhausted but optimistic that this was an anomaly and now it's over. We celebrate with pizza and a movie. Hoping for calm, I work to get back my energy, divest my fatigue. I resume running, see friends, relax during a massage. I have no idea this is a prelude.

The god Indra lives in a heavenly palace adorned with a magnificent net of jewels. Each knot of the net has a jewel attached and each jewel reflects all the others. In each reflected jewel is the reflection of every other jewel. All of the jewels sparkle in many colours when one jewel moves in the breeze. When one knot moves, it creates a great ripple effect.

When my daughters and I are happy together, we refract glittering happiness. So it is. Like jewels, sparkling ripples of joy.

But when Alessandra is angry, I hear, I feel the beating of drums. So much seems stacked against her. Her life is a perpetual battle. I am angry with her and for her. I swallow this anger, push it down deep in my chest, but still it rises to bang against her own.

Alessandra's adolescence is marked by crises, hospitalizations, self-harming incidents, suicide attempts, three periods spent in comas resulting from suicide attempts. At home, chaos governs life. I am fretful for Renata, on high alert, anticipating.

When Alessandra is fourteen, I enter her bedroom. . .

She barely responds to me when I speak and when she does, she slurs.

I see the empty containers of her medications. I lift, drag, pull her to the car, to the hospital where she collapses at the entrance. Her stomach is emptied, and she is taken to the intensive care unit.

She is fifteen. . .

Unaware of an egregious side effect of a recently prescribed medication, I find Alessandra in her room frantically banging her arms, her wrists, her body against a wall. In the emergency unit, she is given a medication to counteract her reaction to the medication.

At times Alessandra sends me notes.

*Dear mum, nothing helps. I'm feeling a lot of emotional pain.*

*Dear mum, I WANT TO END THE PAIN.*

*Dear mum, I'VE HAD ENOUGH OF LIFE. Good bye. I want you to know this is the best thing I can do for myself. This pain is too much to bear. You will always be in my heart, just understand this is the best. I don't want you to feel sad for me. It's what I want. I will be pain free.*

*Dear mum, I know I'm in and out of reality. What can I do? I want to have a normal life.*

*Dear mum, I made a decision I'm not going to live anymore because I will never be hospitalized again. I learned talking to a doctor gets me nowhere. I love you so much and I know you love me so much. I don't want you to cry. I truly believe as a mother and daughter we will meet and you're like a beautiful flower in my heart. I want it to be this way. When I won't be around I will carry that beautiful flower in my soul.*

*Dear mum, DNR. Give away all my organs but not my heart. I want to keep those I love in it. I want to be burned in the clothes I have on.*

# Home

## First, again

My mother didn't tell stories about her past. But this much I know. The fifth of seven: sister Jessie succumbing to illness at two years; her eldest sister Lyda, in her twenties killed by a car while on a ski trip with girlfriends; a father dead from a heart attack at forty-five; a younger brother, George, dead in his early thirties from an intransigent form of arthritis; and her mother ill for years, dead three months before I was born. My mother's remaining brother and two sisters, reeling from shared tragedies, stayed close, never marrying.

A Protestant, my mother married a Catholic, newly arrived from Scotland, a man her siblings never warmed to. This man, my father, felt a need to suppress his Scottish accent, worked hard and often late, and often returned home angry. But he loved to sing and make puns, rarely drank alcohol, and left the upbringing of my sister and me to my mother. Like her, he never told us stories of his life.

My mum, Irene, sweet-natured and competent, never spoke about dreams she may have had, and I never asked. She did, though, tell me that she had miscarried three times before my sister was born. And when I was thirteen, as she and I were sitting in our backyard, she told me she wanted to leave our father. I didn't ask her why and she might not have told me in any case. Her reason remained a mystery and she never followed through. She died at sixty-eight and left her husband bereft and her children crushed.

Our house was a house of secrets, where the religious clash between the two extended families meant we tried at different times to please both, and truth often shifted. My family held tight its code of secrecy, *how life was*.

In contrast, I resolve to tell my children and my friends about my dreams, what I stand for. I want to be transparent to those I love. I fail to consider how difficult this might be for one so ill-prepared, without model or example. And when trouble comes, I rationalize, hold it back from my friends. This is Alessandra's life, I tell myself, it's not for me to talk about; no one will understand. I will be judged. I'm scared. I'm embarrassed. Worse yet, I'm failing.

# Home

## Tense

Renata shines at soccer and volleyball, treasures her collection of books, writes poems and stories, and excels in drawing designs of dresses, skirts and evening gowns. She sews clothes for dolls, for herself, and for me. The day before her first day of high school, she carefully plans out her clothes.

That day, heading to the storage area in a corner of our basement, I leap back at the sight of a noose hanging from a rope around a steel rafter. Shaking, I cut it down with a ladder and knife. I say nothing to Renata and I wait for Alessandra to come home.

But she doesn't. Renata goes to bed early. Still Alessandra's not home. I call houses where I hope she might be. I call hospitals, call the police. Still later, someone from a gas station calls to tell me she's there, confused. When I find her, we go to the hospital, where after several hours, she's admitted. Once again, reality has escaped her.

Deciding to wait until the afternoon to tell Renata that her sister is in the hospital, the next morning I drive Renata to her first day of high school. This, my effort to shield her from yet another crisis in the long line of crises.

# Home

## As in

Again, Alessandra is admitted to a psychiatric unit, and this time when she is discharged, I know, I just know, she won't get sick like that again. Her past childhood trauma will burn itself out and she will leave behind its effects. She has her future. My love and our bond will keep her well. In July, I rent a cottage beside the ocean in New Brunswick for two weeks. I look forward to strolls along the shore, to the sunset over the ocean, to a captivating book.

Five days before the end of our holiday, Alessandra experiences symptoms and tells me she's getting sick. I try not to show panic and resolve to keep her close, not let her wander. But the next evening, she disappears from our cottage. Frantic, I go in search of her and see her swimming in the ocean far from shore. No one nearby. As I call, she continues to swim farther away from me, farther into the sea. Dusk descends and I strain to spot her as she becomes smaller and smaller until just a dot, then nothing. Darkness has engulfed the sea.

Renata is in the cottage and I silently beg her not to come outside. I wait in the dark, calling, "Come back come back!" I see only night all around me but I keep calling, "Hurry, come back," until from the shore a distance away I hear Alessandra's voice.

Back in the cottage I lock the door and put chairs against it to warn me if Alessandra starts to leave during the night. She remains in a psychotic state for the rest of our holiday. Arriving home, I bring Renata to a neighbour's home and I take Alessandra to the hospital, where she's admitted.

My hope crumbles, though I still hold tightly onto pieces of it. Surely, this time is the last.

At sixteen, Alessandra is clear: "I don't want to have mental illness or hyperactivity. I want to be happy and feel good about myself."

That summer she loses her best friend.

The Weimaraner, the silver spirit, strong, intelligent, protective of its family members. A dog to keep us safe, and Kuzka does, for thirteen years. While Alessandra rollerblades and bicycles, Kuzka runs alongside. They watch baseball together in the park and Kuzka waits on the sidelines as Alessandra plays basketball in the same park. When they are outside together, I don't worry. Then that summer, she and I sit on the floor as Kuzka, her best friend, is euthanized. Alessandra holds Kuzka's head while our silver spirit takes three breaths, then none.

Yet, that same summer

The wild birds brought to the Wild Bird Care Centre are injured, ill, or orphaned, and they are distressed to be there. Alessandra works at the Centre during the summer, arriving early, staying late, never flinching at the sight of a bird with injuries, never fearing the wrath of a bird frantic in pain. She talks softly to the birds and they like that. When a bird regains its health and is about to be released from the Centre, she says "Goodbye, Godspeed."

Alessandra graduates from high school and two years later she will graduate from college.

Following her college graduation, a family friend invites Alessandra for a celebration dinner at a restaurant. Bringing her home, he stops in a deserted park by a river where he sexually assaults her.

I don't press charges. In the bitter landscape of he-said, she-said, the legal system can steamroll over and crush a young woman with mental illness. Easy to disbelieve a young Black woman who has already spent months in a psychiatric ward. Easier to believe a charming, white, professional male, an adult admired by many. I burn for justice, but know a court case would only lead to greater pain.

# The Mother

## Passing

She acts as though everything is fine, but her world is anything but that.

The texture of her daughter's mental illness seeps into the mother's life, coils itself around her, and with its way of bending life, shifts her emotional landscape. How to remember her own needs, how to keep her family from toppling psychologically, how to right the straitjacket of mental illness.

How to stanch exposure of her inner self, the loss of safety, the isolation of the loss. More secrets. More than ever, she feels she must go silent. Buried by the effort.

Her focus curves to stem crises, create new meaning within the shedding of dreams. How to fit in the world, hold burnout at bay, unlearn, learn?

Abandonment, hyperactivity, learning disabilities, mental illness—the mother tries to shield the signs and symptoms behind the living room curtain. It takes surprising strength to keep that curtain closed. The window's always blowing open. What can the mother do, how can she ameliorate these unpredictable storms?

She feels fragile. She grasps at moments of joy, leaps to appreciate those occasional moments of ordinary behaviour, feels grateful even for foibles. Surely things will work out? She wants to back up time, push the effects of mental illness out of the house, so she pretends, resists, tilts away, and refuses to face the sorrow head-on. How can she speak to others of this pain when she assumes they'd have the same reaction? Assumes they would look past her, tilt away, discreetly, firmly, shut the window.

She sees a psychiatrist for six months. Then, two years later, she sees a psychologist for eight months. Later, she sees yet another psychologist. Easier to talk to someone who won't judge, who won't spread the word about her daughter, about her. Her story may taint others' feelings. Mental illness looms that powerful.

Each day she wakes up tired. She's cautious with others, uncomfortable, afraid they might ask how her daughter is doing. Where would she begin? How to acknowledge her pain to herself, navigate the world around her, how to tell her story? Will the telling spoil her daughter's chances at a decent life? Perhaps if she stays quiet, the problem will go away. Maybe the mother's quiet will buy her daughter's escape from this turmoil. Maybe that's the tradeoff.

She's aware she's drowning, yet doesn't want weakness, needs to keep on, wants things better, way better. But her hope is cracking.

Mostly she feels flat. When not held down by numbness, three feelings dominate her emotional life. A continual rotation – anger, sadness, grief.

# The Mother

## Disseverment, spilling

Mental illness dissevers, unhinges, leads to self-doubt, prompts one to question oneself despite inadequate answers. The mother becomes familiar with how the effects of mental illness spill into and through a person, into family and friends, strangers, spilling through society, through and beyond the margins of everyday. Making messes, making her explain, making her mop spills, brace herself to mop more spills, explain again, to face others, always explaining. She repairs messes, re-explains, forgives, apologizes. In the residue of the spillages, her life begins to change, becomes defined through them and within them. Other parts of her life appear to her paler, less distinct. Their importance recedes.

Yet, from this effort, uncomfortable as it is, comes an internal shift. She learns to stand in the middle of the spillage, to look straight at the destruction, to face the sorrow head-on. A desperate decision.

She stays the course, knowing there will be more struggle, knowing, at last, that her daughter's mental illness is not going away. For years, she thought each crisis might be the last. Now she knows better.

Epigenetics: the impact of traumatic experiences can last a lifetime, is held in a child's DNA, and may be inherited from one generation to the next.

Traumatic separation from parents: creates toxic stress in a child that can profoundly impact development, harm the nervous, endocrine, and immune systems, can alter DNA, and affect attention, impulsive behavior, decision-making, learning, and cause emotional damage. It can increase the risk of social problems and stress-related diseases, disability in adulthood, and early death.

Environment, nutrition, and level of caring and belonging: link to well-being and mental health.

Chronic trauma: alters a child's brain, makes her overreactive, makes it difficult for her to experience security and may increase the likelihood of developing psychiatric disorders later in life.

Experiencing interfering auditory hallucinations, Alessandra once again enters the hospital. Along a small path at the back of the hospital on a June afternoon, she and I come across two birds loudly calling. "They're really upset. They're saying we shouldn't go any further." Alessandra quickly turns around. "Hurry, Mum, we've got to go."

Shortly after she is released from hospital, I take what will become my favourite photograph of her, standing in the woods looking with joy at two nuthatches, one on each of her index fingers.

Alessandra: I will take care of you when you're old.

Me: Thank you.

Alessandra: I will die before I'm thirty.

Me: Please don't do that.

Alessandra: I don't want to live after you die.

Me: Please keep living after I die.

I have left Alessandra inside a hospital too many times. A desolate feeling, missing someone who should be at home, and so often on a night walking out of a hospital, a wind comes around a corner of the building and catches me. Makes me lonely.

# Home

## If only

I struggle to manage Alessandra's emotional hurricanes as they hit, crashing into the house as though the walls and ceilings of our home are falling inward, the floors shaking unsteadily, one upheaval on the next on top of the next. The shocks toss and heave the foundation of our home, and each time I rally to protect both Renata and Alessandra from the impacts. I press on, and the mental health, housing and social service agencies press hard against me, until I almost buckle. Drained from the dual efforts of supporting and passing, I want one thing only: sleep.

The chaos at home becomes more unbearable and relentless. It's not possible for Alessandra, now twenty, to live at home in the wake of another lengthy hospitalization. The weight of the onslaught of her challenges, her pain, overwhelms me. The chaos would break all three of us.

Following her hospital discharge, a social worker organizes housing for her and she moves to the tenth floor of a YMCA where she is able to stay for three strained weeks.

When I visit, she's confused. She cries. I look around her room. Concrete walls, the scent of transience, her clothes in two garbage bags. I look away from them—the shock of my daughter no longer in her brightly coloured room in our home, her clothes draped over neat hangers. The outside world looks drab through her small window, yet I cling to some hope, telling myself: *This will turn around and we'll look back on this as yes, a despondent period of time, but oh thank goodness, it's passed.*

After three weeks she is re-admitted to hospital and I take her clothes-filled garbage bags from the YMCA. When she is discharged from hospital this time, no housing plan has been put in place, and she has nowhere to go. Late in the evening, after eight phone calls, I find a place for her, an emergency shelter, part of a motel that permits people to stay for three days.

I want her back home but none of us will survive if that happens.

As both girls have grown older, the risks have become too great. What if she brings home a dangerous acquaintance, becomes overtaken by anger, tries to harm herself again? The chaos never stops. Her level of emotional dysregulation has led to constant stress and fears. None of us can function. The cycle has become too much to bear.

I notice the proliferating mental health ads and posters that show off a woman with mental illness who has a smile so wide her face might break. Her smile, perky and beaming, calls out to me. *See how vivacious and upbeat I am. Mental illness isn't such a big deal. Don't I appear healthy and happy? Don't I look as though I have no side effects from my psychiatric medications—no muscle spasms, no brain fog or immense weight gain, no hallucinations, suicidal ideation, stroke, heart attack, psychosis, or sudden death.*

In another newspaper ad, a pretty, respectable-appearing young woman with conservative makeup and adult earrings looks sad. She asks me to donate. *I hate how I look. Why do I feel this way?* Then I read: *Help this hospital to discover innovative ways to prevent and treat mental illness.*

I'm angry at mental illness.

Step by fatiguing step, I lose my ability to concentrate. That, and exhaustion, prompt me to take three weeks leave from work. All I need to recuperate is to sleep plentifully and I'll bounce back replenished. But I don't bounce back; instead I'm even more enervated. My leave stretches well past those weeks and again I see a psychiatrist, who tells me that I'm depressed. Hearing the news, I tell her I can't be. "I've got too much on my plate to be depressed." My leave continues.

# Even the Bones in Her Face

The intense pain seen and heard on each shift, never ending. The quick decisions needed.

It takes me five years before I think about the triage nurse, integral to what occurred, yet beyond the orbit of my mind. I never knew her name, or thought about how the event may have affected her: her level of stress, perhaps guilt, perhaps her career itself.

When I arrived, two police officers were speaking with her. They turned and approached me, told me my daughter had been transferred to another hospital, better equipped to handle the situation. They told me they would meet me there. The nurse didn't look at me; I only saw her back. Did she stay to finish her shift or did she go home after what happened?

My tunnel vision from the shock leaving her out of my focus. Now I wonder if she ever thinks about that day.

This is how it was for me.

Late Sunday afternoon, dark, even for mid-January. I'm home in a comfortable chair, a cup of Yorkshire Gold beside me, a mystery book waiting to be cracked open. I'm trying to relax.

An hour later, I'm in the waiting room of a hospital's intensive care unit.

The room has no windows, off-white walls, a room soaked in small hope. Tissue boxes on side tables stacked on top of a handful of magazines. It's a cramped space and I'm alone there under nagging florescent lights. A note on the desk states that a volunteer will return Monday morning. Three identical grey couches, comfortable enough. I sit at the end of the couch nearest the door, stunned by the news.

The two police officers enter and introduce themselves again, although their names flow past me like a dream. They interview me, both asking questions and scribbling notes on small notepads. I only care that my daughter lives. Like their names, their questions drift in and pour through me, but the description of what happened locks in.

I learn this. The previous day Alessandra felt suicidal and went on her own to emergency, scared of what she might do to herself. After a long wait, she was sent home. She returned the next day again on her own, and after waiting two hours to see a doctor, she asked permission to go outside for a cigarette. Although protocol is to never leave someone suicidal alone, the triage nurse says, "No problem, go ahead. The wait will still be a while longer."

On a third-floor deck, Alessandra casually walks over to its short concrete railing, which looks over a road. Other people on the deck notice her sitting on the railing, dangling her feet, looking down at the road, all seemingly innocuous. Until she leans forward and disappears. She has jumped headfirst from the ledge onto the road beneath.

Bones in her face break. Her jaw. Her shoulder. Elbow. Both wrists. Teeth smash. A kidney separates from its source of blood. There is massive internal bleeding. Her face is unrecognizable.

Several people scream. Someone runs inside to tell the triage nurse.

In the intensive care unit, a physician tells me it is too dangerous to do surgery to try to stem Alessandra's internal bleeding, although that is what is threatening her life. I hear him say my daughter is in a coma and brain damage could be extensive. He speaks bluntly: "She might not make it through the night, but definitely if we operate, she won't survive. Stay here tonight."

I hear myself groan in response and notice I'm crying. Working to take in the information, my mind scrambled from what he has said, I ask him to repeat it a second time. To be certain.

Approaching Alessandra's bed, my footsteps jar over the buzz and hum of monitoring machines. Breathing with oxygen equipment, her face distended, bruised, cut, her jaw held in place, eyes too swollen to open, hair matted with blood and road grit. I sit with her, stare at her face and whisper, "It's me, your mum. Live. Make yourself live. Don't die."

I take breaks back in the empty waiting room where I drink coffee from a machine and stare at tissue boxes and magazines, then return to the intensive care unit. Again and again. All night. My mantra, *Don't die tonight.*

I lose track of time, but walking through the hall between the two rooms, I look out the window. Almost dawn. I see daylight as a release from this nightmare. That she'll stay alive. At 9:00 a.m., I go home. She is still alive.

Walking through my house it feels changed. Or is it me, already changed? The waiting mystery book and the cold tea on the table seem from a previous era. I lay down without changing my clothes and sleep for three hours, then head back to the hospital.

I begin a new routine.

Get up.    Go to the hospital.    Back home.    Hospital again.

The routine continues, each day resembling the previous. I strive to keep it together, to appear in control, to look as though I know the language of medicine. To not cry.

In the intensive care unit, where no one smiles, where it's never quite day, never quite night, in-between life and death, I try hard to meld into its culture. I speak softly.    Walk quietly.    Offer coffee, cookies. Say thank you a lot.    When asked to leave for a few minutes, I leave quickly.    No questions.

On day four, a man in the bed beside my daughter's, dies. On day seven, a woman dies. Day ten, another woman. Day thirteen, a family of three—two teenagers and their mother—sob beside a bed close by.

Again and again, trying not to sound frantic, I whisper to my daughter, *Live, please live.* Yes, she suffers from depression, but when she doesn't, you would never know that she ever had. She doesn't want to die. I have to believe that.

Each day I eat less. Only sporadically does sleep fully let me in.

Especially during the twenty minutes it takes me to get to the hospital, into the elevator and into the waiting room where I buzz the unit, "I'm here, can I come in," the questions hang: Will she emerge from the coma? And if she doesn't? And if she does? No answers. Blank.

On the fifteenth day, as I approach my daughter's bed, the curtain around it closed, something feels amiss, dampened down. I'm suddenly cautious. For the worst. The usual hum and buzz of nearby equipment are gone. I stop and look around. No one looks back at me. All busy with the business of staving off death.

Then behind the curtain, I hear a nurse say my name and I open the curtain and slide inside the small twilight space. The oxygen equipment is gone. Holding back terror, I say hello. Or maybe I just mouth the words.

Then I notice that my daughter is breathing on her own. I lean in towards her, and as I do, I scarcely make out the word, but I do, and in a voice, small, raw, I barely hear her say, mum.

A dead kidney remains in her body. Her bones will heal.

During the war in Vietnam, 54,000 Americans died. In 1987, the United States government identified 102,000 veterans who died by suicide.


Suicide attempt

attempt to imagine

act of

day after

items found

numbness

in her shoes

attitudes toward

psychiatry as

where now

# Home

## Sheltering

My daughter is living at a young women's shelter, but after two weeks she overdoses on her medication and is taken by ambulance to a hospital where she stays for a week. Again, the hospital provides no discharge plan and the shelter won't take her back, as it doesn't accept anyone with possible suicidal signs.

I find her a place at a women's shelter. Although I can leave phone messages for her, for privacy reasons I am not told whether she is there. For several days I leave messages, but don't hear from her. Then I am contacted by shelter staff. Alessandra has slit her wrist and again has overdosed on pain medication. She spends six days in a hospital's intensive care unit in a coma. Once again, there is no housing plan, and once again, she cannot return to that shelter for the same reason as before.

Now she lives at a shelter for men and women where navigating myself past the front entrance, I walk over three men lying on the floor propped against the door, perhaps passed out. The smell on entering stuns me. Thick pungency of unwashed clothes and bodies, cigarettes, and meatloaf, all melded together. The smell attaches itself to me, my jeans, sweater, my shoes, glues to my eyes, rolls into my nose, through my lungs. I try small intakes of oxygen. I want to cough. I want to leave. A desperately bleak place with sorrow lurking in every corner. The women's dormitory is in the same large room as the men's, separated by a curtain. My daughter explains to me that there are fights and screams all night. She's scared.

I'm scared. And sad and riddled with guilt and feeling lost, weak, abandoned by health professionals and social service professionals, stuck with nowhere helpful left to turn for housing, tired of the excuses, *Sorry, there's no space*, tired of hearing about another long waitlist, tired of fighting, tired. And alone.

Where to turn? How to keep going forward, the necessity to not give up, the need to take care, fix this situation. I need help.

She begs me to let her come home. She crosses her heart and promises it will be fine. She cries from despair, from feeling alone at the shelter, from being in a distant and unfamiliar part of town. How could I not allow my daughter to return to the safety of home, to be able to leave this terrifying place? But the situation wouldn't last. Gently, I say, "I'm very sorry, I'll find you a better place, but not home."

The second time I visit her there, a fight among a group of men breaks out and police are called. Four police cars arrive as I drive away with my daughter to wait it out at a nearby coffee shop. I beg the housing placement people to find her another spot, but nothing turns up. Alessandra becomes zombielike, rarely speaking, rarely looking at me directly.

She walks under a bridge where city employees are working a short distance away. They have left open a can of gasoline and she drinks from it. I hear about it when the hospital contacts me. She stays there one month.

A place in a group home for women opens up. My first reaction is relief: not a shelter—a facility. Four blocks from our home, although not at home. But the staff are unfriendly, their tone demeaning, strict, chastising. Stringent rules, no leniency, early curfews, precise times to get up, go to bed. Four women share a small room. Little give and take.

Alessandra and a friend in the facility are permitted to go shopping together and she becomes less sad, even a bit happy. But the rules grate on her and she chafes. "Ignore the unpleasantries," I tell her. "That's all they are." My hope that this residence will last for her remains tight. But a staff member finds an unpermitted razor in her drawer and she's given a warning. The next week, for a reason I no longer recall, the shelter evicts her without warning—no time to find alternate housing. My hope crumbling like sawdust.


At times Alessandra responds to her illness with humour. One day she wears a miner's light on her forehead. Laughing, she tells me it's because she's a brain surgeon. "That's a joke," she says.

# Passing

through places that shift the landscape of our lives even further as passing and passable continue to slip.

## Pass through

meeting rooms for special education, for ADHD consults, for learning disabilities consults; for international adoption support groups, for parents of children with mental illness; offices for housing support, for financial support for people with special needs, for mental health agencies; psychiatric hospitals and psychiatric units of general hospitals, psychiatrists' offices, hospital emergency units, intensive care units; shelters, emergency crisis lines, college support offices for special students; the work world for anyone out of the ordinary.

I set up meetings, lobby on behalf of my daughter. I hope for positive results, for someone to say, *I'll move the system for her.* One time, then another, then another, the systems betray my daughter. I take notes and email them to the people I meet with. "This is my understanding of what was said at our meeting. Am I correct?" No one ever replies. I gladly accept crumbs when offered—a small suggestion, a kind word— and I almost cry if anyone steps out of bureaucracy to understand.

Still trying to pass as a concerned parent but not overly concerned; to appear intelligent but not excessively knowledgeable; to seem assertive, but not overly insistent; to come across as calm and sensible, yet not a pushover. Trying to understand the limitations of what can be done, trying to parse the possibilities from impossibilities. *If only there were a way. But there isn't.* At times I am willing to get on my knees to plead for what my daughter needs. Inside, I want to scream at the wall of indifference. Will no one bother to care, no one try to influence an inelastic system, no one remember a piece of vital information that could help?

# The Mother

is happy    yes sometimes

annoyed    by obvious advice

scared    each time the phone rings late at night, sometimes when
the phone rings any time

sad    most of the time, the feeling leans on her as she leans
against it

tired    when is she not?

# Home

## Forced out

Years ago, while conducting research in West Africa, the mother talked with a school principal on a scorching afternoon. Asking an idle question about the community's local history, she learned that the school stood on the site of a former holding fort where captured children, women, and men were imprisoned before been taken to ships to cross the Atlantic Ocean as part of the slave trade. Before being transported to Brazil, her daughters' ancestors would have been kept in a fort in West Africa. The mother suspected that these ancestors may have stood on the exact spot where she was standing. She yearned to hug her children, to hold them close.

Her children are teenagers now, and she no longer conducts research on the effects of violence on war-affected girls. That work for her is finished. With one daughter's life in tatters, there is only so much truth she can bear.

# Home

## Solitary

Placing a person in solitary confinement is tantamount to torture.

The primitive nature of incarceration due to illness.

Nelson Mandela and John McCain stated that solitary confinement was the worst part of prison.

A mentally ill man in solitary confinement doesn't get his medication. He pleads for it and desperate, he hangs himself. He is cut down by guards.

Apart from my divorce proceedings—straightforward and quick—I've never been in court. This time I wait, the muscles of my face tight. *Remember*, I caution myself, *keep an optimistic posture.* Thankfully, few people are in the courtroom.

When my daughter's name is called, I scrunch my face to hold back tears. I hear a side door at the front of the room open. I hear movement and I force myself to turn my head toward the door. My heart lurching, I wonder what will happen if I have a heart attack right now, right here, and I wonder how many people have heart attacks in courtrooms. I watch fretfully as she is brought in, a police officer holding her arm, her wrists bound by handcuffs. A lawyer says something. A judge says something else. The lawyer replies. Back and forth. The judge asks my daughter something, she doesn't understand, her mind is in another place. I search her face, her expression confused, scared. I recognize that expression.

She does not look around the room, doesn't notice me. The officer nudges her arm and they leave. It takes me a minute before I stand up, and as I do, I remind myself to stay composed. I want to be home.

The judge has ordered a transfer to a psychiatric hospital, but there are no available hospital beds, and instead she is transferred to a provincial jail. I am told she has been placed in a solitary confinement cell for her safety.

Alessandra spends one month there. She is allowed outdoors for short periods each day. Although I beg with administration, she receives no psychiatric medication. Rules are set. Why solitary confinement? Because she might attempt suicide while medication to support her mental health is denied.

Solitary confinement, alone twenty-three hours a day. Cold all the time, a canvas gown, a rip-proof blanket on a security mattress. Meals appear through a knee-high slot in the door, and appointments with a jail psychologist take place through the same slot. What of her dignity, self-worth, identity? The results of minimal human connection— monotony, loneliness. Mental disintegration begins after even a short time, and if a person is already suffering from mental illness, what then?

I visit her frequently, wait on a worn-out bench in a decaying room. She enters with a guard standing behind her. She is in handcuffs. A thick glass barrier separates us. During these visits, my mind is in an uproar and I can barely focus my thoughts. I ask her questions. "How are you doing?" "How do you spend your time?" I say, "I miss you terribly. You'll be out soon." I chat about what I'm doing, how her sister is, how our dog is. I'm acting, forcing the words out, because what else to do? But more than anything, I long to hold her. Surely that would help her.

I strain across the glass chasm. The stifling room claustrophobic. Visits timed, and always too short.

Renata visits her sister, and like me, she isn't prepared for the tension, the unfreedom, the monitoring.

On day thirty, I am at the entrance of the jail waiting to pick her up. She walks out and smiles when she spots me, then races into the car. Her psychiatric episode has run its course. We drive home, both subdued. Alessandra recollects only a portion of what happened during her stay. *For the best,* I think, *for the best.*

But I brought it on. I am the reason why she was in jail.

This is how.

The day of her arrest nothing seemed to be going smoothly. My washing machine broke, filled with water and clothes. I was already on edge when call display indicated a private number, code for major problem, a problem that cuts loose immediate plans. The speaker's voice soft, raising my inner alarm. He identifies himself as a police officer.

"Is your daughter Alessandra? We're bringing her to your house. We'll be there in ten minutes." He tells me someone had contacted them concerning a young woman on the highway. I ask him about my daughter. He answers, his voice still slow. "We've just got her into our car, she appears distraught, maybe suicidal."

As my heart thrashes, I tell myself to just breathe normally. I'm outside when they turn the corner. Glancing toward the car, I see my daughter in the backseat, banging her head against the window. I tell them to take her to emergency. After they leave, I go back into the house. My legs feel weak and I steady myself against a wall.

Two hours later the officers return with my daughter—the hospital has refused to admit her. The police are upset. They think she should have been admitted. I'm upset.

They let my daughter out of their cruiser, escort her into the house and leave. No choice. Alessandra follows me blankly through the living room, and shortly after, loping into the kitchen, throws a plate against the wall then punches her arm through the kitchen window. I hold onto her as I grab my phone and dial the police. They need to come quickly. My daughter is strong and her bleeding arm is giving her no hesitation. In a short time, the same two officers arrive.

They bemoan that a jail as a hospital overflow for people with mental illness is a deplorable option, but this is now the only possibility and they offer it to keep Alessandra safe. She's broken the kitchen window. They can arrest her and take her into custody. "No other option," one of them says. I agree. No option.

I sweep up the broken glass. Court next day.

# Home

## Hardly

At twenty-three, Alessandra works at a satisfying job and for a year lives in her own apartment. Then hospital, then a motel that houses the homeless, then, between hospital stays, a friend's living room, then another friend's. Throughout that period, so many hospital stays. Too confusing to count them all. At one, she contracts MRSA, a difficult to treat infection resistant to many antibiotics, and she remains in isolation for a month. Then, at twenty-six, she lives again in her own apartment.

Until

# Home

## High rise

Alessandra has boyfriends. My favourite is Corey. Polite, leaning toward shy, stationed at an American military base just south of the border. Sitting on my couch with his hands clasped together on his lap, he addresses me, *Ma'am*. From Georgia, now slightly out of poverty, he possesses a caring nature. But Alessandra can't hold her mental health together and he can't cope. He leaves to fight a war. No word from him after that. Perhaps by now he has been deployed several times too many. Perhaps now, coping with himself is the best he can manage.

Later, others. Some, not so nice. Some mean. None for long.

Robert teaches me this: If you're compelled to hoard and your apartment becomes unmanageably congested, one solution is to keep that place for storage, move to your girlfriend's, and amass even more newspapers, magazines, old clothes, and random objects there. When Robert moves into Alessandra's apartment, his stuff takes over the space. A thin wriggly path trails through the living room, there's one place to sit, items tower on top of one another, higher and higher. He leaves to collect more things, brings them home, opens a can of SpaghettiOs, eats it cold. He rolls his cigarettes. He needs a new knee.

Alessandra is afraid to be alone. He taunts her.

The spine, thirty-three bones, all stacked one on top of the other. Seven cervical vertebrae near the neck, C1 to C7, twelve thoracic vertebrae, T1 to T12, five lumbar vertebrae, L1 through L5. In the centre, a protected 17 to 18 inches long spinal cord, as thick as a thumb, connects bones to the brain. Thanks to our spine, we hold up our head, we stand, we walk.

When the spinal cord is badly injured, nerve impulses are unable to pass through and paralysis occurs. But wait, sometimes the paralysis is temporary, movement stalled. Maybe it will start up again. But no, it stays that way. Stuck.

Paraplegia: paralysis of legs and body below the arms from an injury to the thoracic or lumbar spine.

It could have been more.

Quadriplegia: paralysis of both legs and arms from an injury to the cervical spine. But it's not.

On the first and cold Saturday in January, Alessandra tells Robert she wants to die. She goes by herself to the emergency unit of a nearby hospital. A doctor sees her, sends her home. The next day, she returns to the hospital, anxious and afraid that she will kill herself. Another doctor sees her, sends her home, where she goes, distraught. Robert says, "If you want to kill yourself, do it. Go ahead."

Alessandra steps onto her fifth-floor balcony. Robert says, "Jump. You might as well."

Alessandra moves to the outside of the balcony ledge. She holds on. Looks down. Looks back. Robert tells her, "I know you can't do it."

Then she's not there. He goes to the living room and rolls a cigarette. Alessandra's best friends, two sisters in the apartment beside hers, walk out the front door on their way to buy groceries. Kay looks to the left. Then Doreen. They both scream. Someone else phones for an ambulance.

Alessandra lays on the ground in the small space between her apartment building and the road. She doesn't move. It is twenty degrees below zero and she has on a t-shirt and jeans, no shoes. Her boyfriend looks over the balcony. He doesn't call 911. He had said to her, *If you want to kill yourself, jump. You might as well.* And she did.

When the police arrive at her apartment, Robert is still there. He leaves the apartment and goes back to his. Kay and Doreen take the bus to the hospital. Her best friends. I meet them when I arrive. They need calming and I calm them. Maybe I need calming, but I can't tell. Alessandra needs me.

Leaning over her bed until I ache, I'm stiff when I finally stand up. I want to be as close as possible to her, want to shield her. I want too, to protect Renata from being that close to the shock. But we are shocked. The world, once again, has changed.

The computer screen beside Alessandra's bed has a tiny arrow pointing to one of her vertebrae. My chest hurts. Maybe I'm holding my breath. I hold her hand. Breathe. The doctor asks her if she can tell when he touches her leg. No, she can't. *Oh please, please feel. Focus hard. Pay attention. Then you'll feel your leg.* But she can't.

Two constables enter and I stagger behind them to an empty room. They have come to interview me. What do I know about her boyfriend? What is their relationship like? I'm bewildered. Then they ask if I think he might have pushed her. Robert had told them he had watched her climb over the railing and jump. The constables are not sure he had merely watched. Someone from the apartment building across the road saw her climb over the railing and saw a man behind her, though he couldn't tell if she had been pushed.

Doreen and Kate come back to the hospital the next morning. Finding their friend semi-conscious was hard for them, they tell me. Neither had slept well the night before. "How can you sleep after you've seen that," they ask me.

After that visit, they don't return.

Alessandra's boyfriend comes to the hospital that afternoon. He doesn't ask how she is. He wants the key to her apartment. But no one gives him the key. He's upset. Two security guards are called to escort him out and Alessandra never sees him after that. She never returns to her apartment and it never becomes clear whether he pushed her.

Her broken spine doesn't recover. Her broken hip isn't fixed. Why bother if she can't feel it, they say, but she does feel it, and lives with severe hip pain. It takes time, but her emotions and her spirit get fixed, then later break again, then get fixed again—more times than I remember.

Eventually, she's transferred to a rehabilitation centre. On one visit, I snuggle in with her in her bed. She has just experienced paraplegia for three weeks. She needs to be cozy, to feel warmth, and I need to hold her. We need connection. With each other, to feel, to feel sort of okay.

After several weeks she is moved to a mental health hospital as an interim housing placement while waiting for one more appropriate. I have a ramp built at the side door of our home so that Alessandra can visit.

After Robert, Alessandra has two more boyfriends. The first is personable, but with addictions that preclude a lasting relationship.

The second, Kevin, is so shy he makes Corey seem bold. Alessandra and he a writ-large attraction of opposites. They spend days together, nights apart, he at his basement room with concrete walls and Alessandra at the hospital. For all the obstacles she faced, she attracts people to her. With all her problems, she keeps trying to live an ordinary life, keeps choosing a future.

# Home

## De facto

Alessandra's room is at the end of a long hall. From her window, she can see a worn industrial building, a parking lot. In one corner of her room, her clothes bunch up in fat waves. Edges of socks and t-shirts peek out along the floor at the shore of sweaters and jeans. In another corner is her electric wheelchair battery and transfer board. Pictures line the wall—of her sister, me, our dog. Notices are taped beside them: bingo next Tuesday afternoon, a church service on Saturday, a smoking cessation group starting soon, please come, a visit by a choir, a calendar from the previous month with a picture of a puppy. For baths, she goes to the geriatric unit, where there is a special tub for those who use a wheelchair. Nurses negotiate this tub for Alessandra once a week, since its availability to other units is not automatic.

Her home. She knows most everyone at the hospital, calls the CEO by his first name, jokes with him and with the cleaning staff. She would have left after the first several months, but there's a waitlist—gasp—of thirteen years, more or less, for the sole facility in the area suitable for a wheelchair-using person with mental illness.

I walk to the hospital to visit her. From my house it takes twenty minutes, sixteen if I walk briskly, twenty-five if I slow my pace, which I do more and more. At the front door, small clutches of patients, some mandated to be with staff, most on their own, shift from foot to foot. A few people call to me. "How are you? Alessandra just went upstairs." "It's cold today, I like your coat." I say, "I'm fine, thanks, I'll go find Alessandra, yeah, it was windy walking over here."

If Alessandra is outside when I arrive, she calls, "Hi, Mum, I want you to meet someone." A young friend with Huntington's disease, a judge, a vet who was a vet. She loves that. "Yes, really, Mum."

"Yes, let's go and get a coffee."

"Okay, that sounds good."

Or, "Let's take a stroll around the building."

"Yes, I'd like to do that."

Or, "Did you remember to bring me some shampoo?" or "I need new socks. They keep getting lost in the laundry here."

"I have the shampoo, and okay, I'll buy you some socks."

Or, "I really need to get out of here. This is no place to keep on living. Why can't I live at home? I really want that."


If only I could do it. But I would crumble like dry toast if she came home.

# The Mother

A friend tells her to let go, stop caring. Would the person suggesting that do it herself? Even know how to do it?

The mother is losing hope. When did the mother start sliding downward, grieving, oozing dread? How to not give up and yet save herself. How?

Her daughter's life choices continue to be more and more restricted: a narrowing of friendships and social possibilities; hospitalizations; frequently-changing medications. Accessing buildings and homes proves formidable; years disappear on housing placement waitlists as possibilities diminish. All the while, Alessandra endures constant physical pain.

Again, the mother asks herself, can love ameliorate the situation? She continues to believe it can, although she does ask the question

but

*She doesn't know her daughter's genetic history.*

Levels of serotonin may be determined by genetics. The gene that sets levels of the enzyme tryptophan hydroxylase is associated with high rates of suicide. Genes for mental disease may put some people at risk. Monkeys brought up without mothers have lower serotonin levels.

*Until the age of eight, her daughter lived in an orphanage without a parent.*

Stability in early childhood is important.

*Prior to her adoption, her daughter suffered from neglect and physical and sexual abuse.*

Abuse in childhood may lower serotonin levels permanently, increasing the chance of suicide.

*That children eat well is a significant indicator of health.*

When adopted, she had signs of mild malnourishment.

*Neurological damage to the fetus, caused by alcohol, drugs, glue, may influence mood disorders.*

Unknown.

The mother can't relax. Her daughter's illness becomes the mother's identity. The mother has a cold sore, acne, stomach tightness, sensitive skin, taut shoulders, stiff neck, headache. She sits, crying with heartbreak. Concentration evades her, and in that grey space of the mind where lighting feels dimmed, she knows she has to save herself, yet she's beyond knowing how.

Again, a doctor tells the mother that she's depressed. She takes medication, but it doesn't help.

Do depression and grief conflate? She wonders if she will ever finish grieving. How?

For the mother, the meaning of hope changes. She grasps hungrily at small successes, mourns losses along the way as the family moves into new landscapes, different terrain. She holds together conflicting feelings—acceptance and frustration; sadness and sweetness; love and anger; missing and relief; and guilt, plain and simple.

Worn down, she loses count of hospitalizations. Tension continues, never letting up. How dare she be depressed? She begins to suffer panic attacks, anxiety, a fear of elevators. Is she burned out? How to balance care and attention between her two daughters? How to disclose her world to anyone.

She and her daughters live as hostages.

**Friendly advice I receive to cure my depression:**

*Go for a walk every day*

*Have a massage*

*Force yourself to get out of bed. Be energetic*

*Rest*

*Don't worry. Even psychiatrists don't have good answers around mental illness*

*Watch funny movies. Laugh.*

**Not so friendly advice:**

*You can get over it if you want, just try.*

On my birthday, Alessandra and I eat at a restaurant with juke boxes at the benches. We're the last people there that evening and we jive with the waitress and the cook to the rock and roll music, up and down the aisles. Soon after, Alessandra joins Propeller Dance, an integrated dance group that performs to audiences each June. After her first performance in front of a large audience, she claims nervousness. By the third year, following a dance performance with her group, she wheels to the centre and front of the stage and with her group in a semi-circle behind her, sings a capella "What a Wonderful World." I sit among the audience hugging the roses I brought to give her.

# Home

## Turbulent

The surface of memories can remain undisturbed like remnants of a fossil wedged into rock, preserved in the earth's crust unobserved. But when at last noticed, the fossil's outline can bring to light a clear impression of a once-living organism. Teasing out wedged memories can bring up emotions that had crawled away to hidden recesses, small remnants.

I have nightmares.

Night after night men threaten me in my sleep: thugs chase me down dark rainy streets, aiming to slit my throat; murderous marauding gangs surround me as I startle myself awake, a group of masked assassins wielding hunting knives encircles me with the intent to stab me to death.

In daylight, I grapple with how to defeat these faceless men, yet the nightmares continue. Each morning, sagging exhaustion.

For a month, these men continue to attack, until I spot my own guilt, the guilt that I might want to tell secrets I've held so long to protect my family from censure, judgment. I'm hemmed in by guilt, wrapped in culpability, strangled by my childhood belief that it's dangerous to tell too much, that keeping secrets maintains safety. The code of secrecy I learned as a child is fighting back to keep me in obedience.

That very night, I am held prisoner in a dank room within a compound, and the murderers' intent to kill me is clear. Aware that I'm near death, I grab the covered face of one of the killers and scream. "You let me out of here and do it right now!" He jumps back and I walk out of the compound.

The nightmares end.

Still, my failure. I save myself from these murderers, but I'm not saving Alessandra, who has her own thoughts and fears, and possesses a rhythm of her own.

# Home

## A sort of

The social worker hesitates, lacking the mettle for her job. She doesn't provide a room for our meeting about Alessandra's housing situation. She shrugs her shoulders. "We'll meet in Alessandra's room," and we do meet there, even though Alessandra has a roommate.

The nurses often speak sharply. They're ill-disposed, at times rude. One day, I tell Alessandra that I'll be there soon to visit. She's happy, looking forward to seeing me.

On entering the ward, a nurse tells me, "Go and wait on the couch outside the unit, I'll come and talk to you in a few minutes." When she returns, she says Alessandra has been rude to her, so she won't allow her to see me. She is punishing my daughter for bad behaviour.

That evening I write a letter to the hospital's CEO. What else to do? He ought to know this.

I never receive a reply.

# Home

## Finding

A person with paraplegia, mental illness, and traumatic brain injury needs a specific kind of housing. Facilities are scarce. Options shrink further for a place to call home.

> The hidden homeless couch-surf, live in unhygienic and unsafe buildings, in overcrowded conditions, sleep in a car or in an interim facility such as a hospital.

A hospital.

> Six years in one, one year in another. Little prospect of permanency.
>
> How hope becomes defined more cautiously, her future, not the usual.

For seventeen years, I struggle to find a home for Alessandra, who moves between apartments, YMCA, shelters, group home, motel, hospitals. Now, at twenty-eight she is being moved into a long-term care facility where the median age on her wing is eighty-six.

# Home

## Barely

The staff on her wing of the long-term care facility are all overworked. Some are discourteous. Several are verbally abusive. The food is soft, mashed, bland. One resident—Alessandra—is under the age of eighty-three. Her nervous roommate is eighty-nine. Alessandra can't choose when to wake or when to go to sleep. Mornings begin by 7:30 a.m. After 7:00 p.m., everyone must whisper; curfew is at 8:30 p.m. She can't even talk on a cell phone after 9:00 p.m. This is a place of little agency or joy.

Alessandra wants music, she wants to spend her days outside with friends, not in an institution eating a desultory lunch, a tasteless dinner. She doesn't want to have to whisper in the halls after seven. Doesn't want to go to bed at nine. The building was designed for older residents, and most staff members prefer the pace of the elderly. Although a few connect with Alessandra's exuberance, she doesn't fit in.

One evening she arrives back at the facility at 10:00 p.m. and is told to apologize to all the staff, which she does.

While waiting for an appropriate facility, she's shamed simply for being young. Some residents make it clear she doesn't fit in, that they would prefer an elderly resident, not her. Living here, she is considered a lower priority for housing and her name stalls on the waitlist. Others in more urgent need take available spots before her. Always someone more urgent on the list. Nothing to do about this quandary.

She lasts one year, eleven months. Twice she is rushed to emergency due to a medication dispensing error, twice for urinary tract infections, the last time for a mental health crisis. Within three weeks she is fine, but the administration has the right to give a person's room away after an absence of three days, and that is what they do.

# Home

## Not possible

A housing social worker suggests another facility, a women's residence for fifty previously unhomed women. I tour it. The facility exudes warmth, but they are unable to provide the level of physical care required for someone in a wheelchair, and Alessandra is not accepted.

I then tour the most appropriate facility, where the waitlist is approximately thirteen years, more or less. At the door of each room is a small memory box into which residents can place an object. The director tells me, "This is to remember that they had a life before they came here."

At a meeting with social workers, Alessandra, and myself, we discuss this facility. After eight years on its waitlist, I'm surprised to be informed that *two* waitlists exist, one public, the other shorter one, private. No one, during all that time, had ever told me about a private waitlist for people willing or able to pay the housing cost. Alessandra suggests a long-term hospital in the city is the best place for her because, as she says, her physical issues will mean she will be placed there at some point in any case. Her application is put forward but not accepted, as her medical needs are not considered complex enough.

At the next meeting to discuss housing, Alessandra comments, "I want a place where I'll have good care." About her time living at the hospital, she says, "It has its ups and downs. Sometimes I like it, sometimes I don't – just like any normal person." At that moment, a nurse interrupts the meeting. Someone is there to take Alessandra to have an x-ray. She calls out, "I'm busy right now. I'm in a meeting— about my life. Tell them to come back in an hour."

# Home

## Another sort of

Because she's not permitted to return to the long-term care facility, Alessandra's home continues to be a room in the mental health unit of the hospital where she was admitted three weeks earlier and where she waits. And waits. Everything she owns is crammed into her small space, in this sort of home. What to do there? The activity centre has four decks of cards, none complete, a ping pong table with warped rackets and sagging net, a TV never off, and board games missing essential parts.

For several weeks, Alessandra rolls herself out of her hospital bed at night. Two creative nurses hunt down enough pillows so her landing on the floor is soft and they let her sleep there. When a friend of hers is suicidal and at the hospital's emergency unit, Alessandra stays with him in the waiting room. A nurse from her ward asks her to return there to take her medication, but she tells the nurse that when she had gone to emergency feeling suicidal, no one was there with her. The nurse returns and gives Alessandra her medication in the waiting area.

On an afternoon radio show, a journalist describes walking down a private airport runway to meet his guests. At the end of the runway are fourteen people in wheelchairs. He walks towards them, watching them watch him as he approaches. They are about to experience paragliding for the first time. Some are elated, others nervous. They glide.

Imagine.

# The Mother

## Off balance

The mother walks along the river near her home where hundreds of inuksuit, works of stones balanced over other stones, stand in the shallow waters of the river. Late each year, the ice disassembles them, but until then they stay steady, balanced. Along the same river in the past, log drivers balanced on rolling logs down the wild water, fighting rapids, log jams, the rush of timber and black flies and the possibility of being crushed. Holding balance kept them alive.

What the mother misses:

the meaning of it all ... the way it once was ... the softness of light

a full moon in a sky bigger than an ocean ... her fourth-grade teacher

play for fun ... time ... one hour yesterday somehow ... focus

She drives past her exit ... wanting to be home ... missing.

She sees a psychiatrist. *Help, I'm steeped in failure. I'm drowning in fatigue.* How to support, stay the course.

Long-term stress causes headaches, digestive problems, suppressed immune system, anxiety, sleep problems, reduced memory and concentration, depression, strokes, heart attacks.

The mother again takes an SSRI. Then a different SSRI. Negative side effect. She takes another, creepy side effect, and another, paranoid effect. She gives up on them, but she's desperate. At the mercy. She loses weight, interest. Exhaustion strains against her body, bringing on headaches and more exhaustion. She forgets about friends. She cries, sleeps.

Her life pulls apart until she's finally stuck.

But stuck comes in other ways too.

# Stuck

Friday afternoon, rush-hour traffic, and a February snowstorm fills the sidewalks with uneven heaving snow. Slush spits from the wheels of cars, hitting the path of pedestrians.

In her wheelchair, its battery wet and refusing to turn over, Alessandra considers her situation. It's not likely that anyone can push her and the three-hundred-pound wheelchair through the snow very far. Wet snow piles like a serving plate onto her lap.

Electric wheelchairs often break down, especially in winter. Once, she might have called for a quick repair. But those days are gone. A new directive requires two quotes before approval. The office closed half an hour ago for the weekend. It will be days before Alessandra's chair will work again. Even in the best-case scenario.

Stuck.

Maybe it wasn't the best idea to have gone outdoors, she considers, but she left five hours ago. It wasn't snowing then. And a restlessness, a craving to move, to get out, to be a part of city life had set upon her. Putting on her turquoise ski jacket, matching gloves, and head band, she took a bus to a friend's apartment. By the time she finds herself back on the street, the storm has come on. Cars move like hips swaying to a slow dance, their wipers ladling snow from one side of their windshields to the other. Pedestrians judder like marionettes, arms out stiffly for balance. One block from her friend's place, her wheelchair lurches slightly before stopping completely.

Stuck.

An accessible bus requires reservations. You need to call before 8:00 a.m. the day of the scheduled drive. An accessible taxi costs more than the $2.00 she has in her pocket.

Pedestrians, hunched in their own worlds, scuttle by. No sign of the snow letting up. Soon, it smothers the bright turquoise of her jacket.

Twenty cold minutes later, a young woman stops. "I can call your mother," she offers.

I come with cash for an accessible cab. We wait an hour before it arrives. By then, the situation is even more precarious. But the driver stops and somehow four of us, all sliding in the snow, push the heavy wheelchair toward the cab.

Cars squeeze and skid around us as we shove the chair up the steep ramp into the taxi. Out of the cold, but stuck without a functioning wheelchair until the following week.

# Home

s

First home, unknown

Then, at two or three, orphanage, until age eight

Family home

Children's hospital, medical unit, psychiatric unit—six
months, two months, three months, four weeks, and more

YMCA, three weeks

Young women's shelter, two weeks, evicted

Women's shelter, two weeks, evicted

Emergency motel for people who are homeless, two nights

Shelter for men and women, thirteen nights

Adult hospital, intensive care unit, psychiatric unit, five
months, three months, three weeks, two months, and more

Group home, bedroom shared with three women, five months,
evicted

Another hospital, psychiatric unit—one month, two weeks,
six years, intensive care unit, medical unit

Another hospital, intensive care unit, three weeks, and more

Rehabilitation hospital, one month

Long-term care facility, one year eleven months

Another hospital, two weeks, eleven and a half months,
one week, four weeks, and more

And

A friend's apartment, one week

Another friend's apartment, two nights

Institutions visited, in hope:

Four long-term care facilities, dingy

Group home for physically differently abled adults, not accepted

Facility for adults with mental and physical health issues, waitlist thirteen years

Facility for women with mental health issues, waitlist long

The most suitable facility for Alessandra now informs us that she is not an appropriate fit there.

Alessandra has moved and moved. She's moved in the face of early childhood abandonment and trauma, neglect, child physical and sexual abuse, learning disabilities, ADHD, mental illness, disabling suicide attempts, traumatic brain injury, paraplegia, diabetes, sarcoidosis, arthritis, pressure ulcers. She has been locked in an orphanage, in hospitals, in a jail. But not in her spirit.

Diagnoses are presented, retracted, changed. None is definitive. Through shifting diagnoses, her life possibilities taper, yet she remains determined, persistent. She doesn't give up. Forefronting loyalty and hope, she engages, lives with joy—except when she doesn't want to live. My work of advocating for her accumulating needs can overwhelm. Often frustrates me.

Her diabetes is insufficiently controlled. Physical pain, constant, severe; psychiatric drugs, trial, errors, side effects. At the mercy of multiple medications, new drugs and old. At the mercy of an illness she wants to be released from. Drugs change. New mixes. Trial and error. Little mercy for errors.

*Psychiatric meds help, don't they?*

*Maxed out on Ritalin, Effexor, olanzapine, lithium, sertraline, loxapine, Ativan, Risperdal, Novolin, epival, trazodone, Avandia, metoprolol, gabapentin, Seroquel, trazadone, atorvastatin, furosemide, metformin, ramipril, diltiazem. To name but a few.*

*And what choice?*


My sadness shifts along a plane to anger. How close they are. It confuses.

Within the now amplified chaos of ongoing and changing needs, Alessandra's options narrow further. I trip, regain balance, hang on.

Most assuredly, I have now lost count of her hospitalizations.



The newspaper reports that a man has shot himself in a washroom on the ward where my daughter is living. The story focuses on how shocked this left the visitors who were on the ward at the time. The story does not mention the reaction of other patients, who may have known the man, been his friend, who may have felt suicidal themselves, who consider the ward their current home.

# Home

## Hospital

Alessandra's next home becomes a room in a mental health ward of yet another hospital, her new home an even tighter space

where she languishes.

A ward like this can damage one's spirit and emotions. I listen to overworked, burned-out staff as they insult patients, infantilize them, ignore their questions. I watch them walk past. The bar for caring is low.

Life with thin purpose, marked by waiting—to be transferred into bed, out of bed, for medications, for her catheter to be changed, for meals, for appointments, for visitors, for a phone call, for the locked unit door to be opened so she can enter or leave, for fresh air, for a proper home. How to live with thin purpose? Alessandra remains here for eleven and a half months. This is where she dies.


The barbarism of mechanical restraints. A patient, my daughter, strapped down to a bed, sometimes two, three days at a time. Such use of force, such violence on a shattered mind.

Hypermasculine security guards, young, muscled men in black uniforms with SECURITY printed large on their shirts, patrol Alessandra's ward. Who would be comfortable in their home, watched by these big men? They roam the halls, moving around with fearsome authority. They don't smile. They are not trained to work with people who have mental illness, and I worry. The atmosphere so tense, so disconcerting. The possibility of common, everyday brutality hangs.

Alessandra knows the sounds:

> of a helicopter flying low. She watches as they transport someone on a gurney out of the helicopter, its wings circling more and more slowly. They move across the street into the emergency unit
>
> of the night footsteps in the hall, who owns them
>
> of the hospital codes over the intercom: blue, white, yellow
>
> of the birds who live behind the hospital, she can find them among leaves, can sing back to them in their language
>
> of my tone, even when I try my best to be cheerful
>
> and she knows the language of dogs.

Her physical pain from arthritis, broken bones, complications of diabetes, from spreading bed sores is chronic and severe. I can barely stand it.

I visit my sister in Victoria for a week, but I don't contact Alessandra for four days after I return. I need time before I dive back in.

When I call, she's angry. I visit.

A friend phones. He's crying after visiting Alessandra. "Such an awful situation," he tells me. I comfort him. Another friend says it's too hard for her to visit. Another friend says Alessandra phones her. Please ask her to stop. And another, "I'm telling tales out of school. Alessandra doesn't give her cigarettes to the hospital staff to keep like she is supposed to."

An old friend from out of town comes with me to the hospital. We go with Alessandra for a walk on the grounds of the hospital. It's hot and humid and I'm impatient.

When I am asked how she is, I don't know how to reply.

I write a second and final letter to the hospital's CEO. A part of it:

*My daughter is currently a patient on the acute care psychiatric ward. She has been a patient there for ten months. This is an extraordinary length of stay on this ward and I am not convinced her multiple needs can be met adequately in acute care. She reportedly has brain damage which is said to contribute to her psychiatric symptoms, but to date no neurologist has been involved in her treatment plan.*

Burnout: a common response to coping for a long period of time. feelings of chronic fatigue, lack of interest in life, lack of self-esteem, headaches, insomnia, depression, and stress-related illnesses.

Ambiguous loss in mental illness: losing a person's personality, how she had been. Her potential, dreams, future, her independence all altered. The loss ongoing, chronic. Ambiguous grief, too, ongoing, chronic.

Ambiguous grief exhausts me, leaves me vigilant, with anxiety, anger, and shame. No relief, no way out, fear and panic replacing hope. My phone stays by my bed. I don't invite friends to my home. I no longer host dinner parties. I don't feel passable.

Nevertheless, I decide to have Thanksgiving dinner at my home with Alessandra, Renata, and two of their friends. Alessandra asks me to make cocktails. "Sure, they're called FTRN." No one inquires about the acronym, and I chuckle as I pour each one a glass of Freakin' Tense Right Now. During dinner Alessandra tells me she is experiencing symptoms. Nevertheless, we each give a Thanksgiving speech. I show everyone a picture of Alessandra and me when she was eight years old. Her boyfriend, Kevin, says, "It's nice to meet such nice people. Thank you for letting me come for dinner."

He leaves with leftover ham, potatoes, and cake, and Alessandra takes an accessible taxi back to the hospital.

# Newspaper Headlines

*Suicidal teen discharged for lack of a hospital bed*

*Coroner's office orders review of Indigenous teen's care at hospital*

*Antidepressants may boost risk of early death: study*

*Long-term care is in "absolute crisis"*

*Suicidal man turned away from hospital*

*Inmate who hanged himself had history of mental illness*

*Hospitals see more youths for self-harm*

*Leaving her son at government office only way for mother to get help*

*Mentally ill prisoners still go straight to the 'hole'*

*Mental health cuts put police in front-line role, psychiatrist complains.*

# Home

## Christmas

On Christmas Day, Alessandra is not well enough to come home. I pack mashed potatoes, sweet potatoes, a salad, baked turkey breasts, apricot juice, a small chocolate cake and five wrapped presents. I add paper plates, forks, spoons, plastic glasses, and Christmas napkins in a cardboard box covered in cheery wrapping paper. At 9:00 a.m., the hospital's main floor atrium is empty, except for Renata, Alessandra, and me. I place a small tablecloth on a round table in the middle of the room and bring out the food. We eat, open gifts. We might be any typical family on a typical Christmas morning. Almost. An hour later, the carboard box repacked, we stuff Alessandra's presents onto her lap and spend a short time in her room. Renata and I drive home, satisfied that somehow we have made the most of it. We have carried on a family tradition, however crookedly. For the rest of the day, I read a book, and Renata goes to a friend's place. At 8:00 p.m., Alessandra phones. Christmas dinner at the hospital was delicious. For a moment, I smile.

Six months later, we go to ground.

Mental illness robs us of all semblance of normality. It steals the cheer of celebrations and relaxed communication. It marginalizes us. I need to recover, but I'm depleted, so bereft and tired that the landscape of my mind becomes surreal.

It's early June and the world spins around me at an unsafe speed, heralding the chaos of the next five months.

Thursday morning 8:00 a.m. Alessandra phones. She's left her dental card at my place and needs it for an appointment in another hour. Her jump four years ago from outside the hospital emergency unit damaged her teeth. It hurts to eat and her teeth desperately need fixing. It will cost $7,000 just for one side of her mouth, and dental insurance won't cover it. The other side can—will have to—wait.

Her wheelchair needs adjustments.

It's been so long since her toenails were cut, they curl and wrap under her toes, and because of her diabetes, they must be cut professionally. No one told me hospital staff are not responsible for this job. The appointment is urgent. I find someone to trim her toenails.

Alessandra's glasses have broken. Her vision has changed and she needs a new prescription. Two days after getting new glasses, they fall to the floor and break. Three weeks after I've had them repaired, they break again. Her eye doctor's office leaves me a message that the temple for her glasses has arrived and I can bring her glasses to the office and come back to get them when they are ready.

Her hair needs to be done and most salons can't accommodate a person in a wheelchair. "Will you find where I can go to get my hair done?" A hairdresser comes to my home, washes Alessandra's hair in the kitchen sink as she leans back in her wheelchair, and then trims her hair in the living room.

She has no toothpaste and needs a new toothbrush. She needs diabetic socks, a pair of shoes, a bus pass, cigarettes.

Physiotherapy treatments are essential.

Renata visits Alessandra and notices that her feet are swollen. There's a smell of urine. She's gained weight.

She wears a wrist brace from being fitted in a wheelchair the wrong size while waiting a week yet again for her own wheelchair to be fixed. Her swollen wrist throbs.

Her new purse is too large to fit over her coat in her wheelchair. It needs to be returned.

A staff member insults her and hurts her leg while helping her dress. What to do?

Her clothes frequently go missing. There's no lock to her cupboard in her room. I buy her new clothes.

Again, she needs diabetic socks. She has been wearing the one remaining pair for four days. Her feet look black, rotting.

Alessandra presents me with a carnation, she tells jokes. It's a sweet visit. "I miss you," she says as I'm leaving. "I miss living at home."

She feels somewhat better, no longer feeling suicidal as she was the previous week.

Concord grapes, her favourite food. Can I bring some for her? A friend tells me she is bringing her some. I'm off the hook.

Renata brings her leg warmers to cover the urine track, otherwise the track is visible.

She notices a group of patients vying for Alessandra's attention. "She's great," they all say.

They say they like her.

During a workshop, police, medical personnel, social workers, and family members wear headphones that simulate auditory hallucinations of voices in their head. The voices are loud, demeaning, officious. The voices insult them and swear at them. Participants are confused and find it extremely difficult to go to a restaurant and write down the menu, to write the words of O Canada, or go to a mall to find a particular item. For some participants these tasks bring on embarrassment.

I buy her an e-cigarette. Six days later it breaks. I buy another one.

She comes home for dinner. She has to leave in the middle of the meal because the accessible bus has arrived an hour early to bring her back to the hospital.

She comes for dinner again. She has been told she can have a bath that evening, so she has to leave before the meal is finished in order to get there in time.

She comes to visit and asks for money for pizza. Asks for a painkiller for her pain. The drugs she's taking don't mask it.

Asks for money for Wednesday's group outing.

Then she has a flu. Her blood sugar levels skyrocket.

Her catheter has given her another urinary tract infection. Her hospital room smells even more strongly of urine. She waits to be transferred to her bed.

A patient attacks her and breaks her foot. No one orders an x-ray until the next day.

Sarcoidosis causes pain in her stomach.

She continues to gain weight. Another concern, but this time I decide not to nag.

The requests exhaust me. Two dollars for coffee, five dollars for something else, sometimes twenty dollars, thirty if it's to buy a birthday present for me. Often the money I give her disappears. She gives it away to others. I look into a public trustee to allocate her funds. I need to unhook from her financial life, but that isn't so easy. I try to keep a lid on the barrage of financial requests, then the lid blows.

My stomach aches with a burning feeling. My head hurts.

A cleaner stops me in the hall. "Alessandra is one of a kind. She's special." Briefly, I'm thrilled.

We pass another cleaner washing the floor. "Hi, Sunshine," he calls out to her.

Alessandra greets another cleaner. "Hi my friend. I miss you. You weren't here yesterday."

We play rummy-o in the unit's activity room. Alessandra tells me she has never been beaten and this game can last two hours. I don't think I can last that long.

I nag her to eat well, to smoke less.

I try yoga. At the end of the class the instructor wishes us peace, love, and ease in body, mind, and spirit. I want to sob and don't go back.

Her right leg shakes uncontrollably. I lean down and place it back on her wheelchair's footrest. Her leg continues to fall off the footrest, grazing the ground. It's dangerous and I'm at a loss how to fix it.

I give her sugar-free candies for her dry mouth. During the visit she offers her cigarettes to a group of people.

Alessandra wants to go out onto the grounds of the hospital with another patient. Permission denied. In frustration, she pushes a table. Again, she is put in restraints.

The next day she phones. "Mum, you have to do something about my situation, please."

If you want to:

Deny a vulnerable group of people the basics for health, including nutritious food and movement.

Steal their potential, their hope, their joy.

Make them wait unconscionable periods of time for transportation and housing.

Render them invisible.

Then you:

Design your psychiatric ward with staff huddled behind locked spaces.

Design your long-term care facility to be at best degrading.

Design your social support system to provide inadequate funding for even essentials.

Design your city and your store, restaurant, and business to deny entry for lack of a small, inexpensive, and portable riser for wheelchair access.

Maintain long housing lists, an unwieldy accessible bus system, winter sidewalks and streets not cleared with mobility and wheelchairs in mind.

Design your culture to look the other way, to keep the general public unaware.

Who will care?

These are some things that happened. Sometimes at breakneck speed.

Alessandra is in her bed. A doctor is talking with her when she is suddenly unable to breathe. She is resuscitated and sent to the critical care unit. The next day when I visit, she looks at me.

"I keep hurting you all the time, I don't want to live anymore. I wish they hadn't resuscitated me. I don't want to be sent back to the ward."

When she is returned to her ward, she says: "I've been put together, how many times?"

I want to know what caused Alessandra's serious cardiac issue. If she had been alone when it happened, she would have died. Her doctor says he doesn't know. "But look at her now. Isn't she doing well?"

How can I get my question taken seriously? Why did her heart stop?

I contact the neurologist who saw her in the critical care unit. He tells me her medications are at a dangerously high level and need to be lowered.


Alessandra's feelings and moods change frequently.

Days one to five: she is cheery and engaging.

Day six: she becomes delusional, asks where she is, apologizes for wrecking people's lives, and asks me if she has killed me. She wonders, "Am I dead?"

Being dead, she says, is a terribly cold feeling.

Day nine: her mood is sweet, tender, loving. Ever so gently, she asks me for a hug.

Day ten: delusional, she is unsure of the season and not sure it is me with her, although she recognizes me by my clothes. She thinks perhaps we're all dead and wants to know if this is true.

Day eleven: calm, her agitation and fear are gone. She invites me to take the bus to the rehabilitation centre so that we could both take the accessible bus home. It warms my heart.

Day twelve: she remains quiet, although somewhat agitated. While not hearing voices, water tastes like gasoline to her, and she can smell gas on her hands, around her.

Day thirteen: she wonders why she had thought that she had been in outer space.

Day fourteen: people's faces look different to her, and she is confused about what is going on.

Day fifteen: in a chatty mood, she talks about how it is for her when she isn't in reality and explains she is anxious then because she thinks someone is going to hurt her. When I ask her what she needs most when she feels like that, she tells me she wants me to visit her more often during those times.

Her glasses break again. This time they can't be repaired.

I wait while a nurse helps her transfer from bed to wheelchair. She again needs shampoo, conditioner, and soap for her shower the next morning. She would like a pair of sandals, she craves a hamburger, she wonders if she can play adapted bocce.

We walk outside, our moods calm, peaceful. Alessandra comments that I take good care of my things. Her consideration makes me realize that I need more compassion and gratitude.

Friendship comes easily to her. "Alessandra's the best," says a young woman with turquoise hair. "Alessandra is fantastic," a teacher tells me. "Although," she adds, "she could tone it down a little." To an elderly woman, Alessandra says, "I like your makeup." The woman smiles, touches her cheek, and sits down beside us. As we leave, Alessandra says, "Sorry, but we have to leave, otherwise we'd like to stay and talk with you."

Her blood sugar levels remain dangerously high.

Alessandra experiences a psychotic episode and continually phones me. I unplug my phone for an afternoon. She wants to leave the hospital.

"Don't go," she pleads, when I tell her I'm going away to a conference for four days. "What if you die there? You can't do this."

I travel to San Antonio and feel lighthearted. I want to dance. Returning home, sadness swallows me. Her doctor reiterates, "Alessandra isn't doing well. She has chest pains, difficulty breathing, her blood sugar levels are not good, and she has another urinary tract infection." They send her for yet more x-rays and a CT scan. When I ask a nurse the results, he asks if I have power of attorney, otherwise he won't let me know.

Her doctor contacts me again. "Alessandra is suicidal and should not be on her own. Her illness will get worse and her brain injury will deteriorate."

A crisis has been building over the last four days. Waiting in her room over an hour to be transferred from her bed to wheelchair, she throws water from a plastic cup and is put in restraints for two days. I arrive to visit, but am not permitted to see her. Again, it has become a privilege for us to see each other.

The art of mixing medications, a cocktail:

*What goes nicely with what? ... How much of each? ... How many can you mix together?*

*Add one, take another away, raise a dose, lower another, keep one the same. For now. ... Try a new one just to see.*

*What might happen. ... makes you dizzy. ... makes your head swirl.*

*Another new one, just to try. ... Head churning. ... Tongue thick. ... Mouth like newspaper. ... Names of meds hard to say.*

*Huge hunger, need to eat. ... Have to have more food.*

*Wobbly. ... Fog all around. ... Slow on the pickup. ... What to say.*

*Feet go forward slowly, heavy to lift. ... Tired, so tired ... sleep all day ... days and more days.*

*Days slip. ... Morning pills slip into tiny plastic cups. Drink up. Swallow. Prove it.*

*Noon pills slip the same. ... Evening, too. ... Night pills slide into some type of sleep, sometimes sort of sleep.*

I get her glasses fixed for the fifth time. I buy her another electric pen cigarette. She has quit smoking cigarettes and I'm thrilled about that. Perhaps my nagging has worked after all. Perhaps things are looking up.

In the midst of a psychotic break, Alessandra doesn't trust the staff. She's terrified. She doesn't eat and doesn't want to take medications. "Do it as a favour to me," I beg. I keep my fingers crossed.

"Do you want me to stay here," she asks. I'm hit by sadness when I look at her wrist bandaged from an attempt.

Kevin is there when I visit on a Sunday afternoon. We all go outside into the sunshine.

Alessandra falls out of bed and lands on her chest. Believing she could walk, it takes a moment before she remembers that she is not able to stand. A chest x-ray is ordered.

She is at the front door of the hospital when once more her heart stops. She is taken to emergency. Later she explains how terrifying it is, not to be able to breathe.

Alessandra is upset by a patient who continues to go into her room when she's not there.

She asks me again, "How will I take care of you when you're old? What good am I?"

Another afternoon I turn off my phone. Again, she is experiencing a psychotic episode and wants to leave the hospital.

Her psychiatrist readministers a standard assessment test on Alessandra, while acknowledging it as a weak instrument to measure her complex psychiatric needs, which change broadly, even within the same week.

Hardly sleeping, barely awake. My sister advises me, "Put your hands over your heart and say to yourself, Donna, I'm here for you."

I try it.

"And what does your frustration feel like?"

*Like pins, like screams, wanting to jump out of my skin, wanting to run away, very far away.*

I put Alessandra's foot back onto the footrest, but my fingers get caught between her foot and the footrest. I curse under my breath as I lift her leg up.

Renata, Alessandra, and I celebrate my birthday with pizza dinner in the hospital cafeteria. The strap of her new purse gets tangled in her wheelchair and rips.

Alessandra's pressure sore isn't healing. It gets larger, scarily so. The open sore causes tremendous pain, and without a catheter during this time, the pain excruciates.

Her psychiatrist tells me she should be able to get in touch with me at any hour, day or night. My phone should never be turned off. Because Alessandra has again attempted suicide and she can only go outside escorted, I should hire someone to take her outside each day. The psychiatrist won't allow her to go the following day to indoor hockey because she would be unaccompanied waiting for the accessible bus and she fears what Alessandra might do.

"And is there no hope for things to get better?"

"This isn't what you bargained for, is it?"

She is the second psychiatrist to say this to me.

*No one bargains for anything,* I think.

*Bad attitude.*

Alessandra won't eat. Food tastes like cadavers. She phones over and over to tell me this. Then her psychiatrist phones. Should she try physical or chemical restraints? "Chemical," I say. The medication will last for three days, and since there will be muscle tautness, another medication will be required to relax the muscles.


Renata, returning home from a Caribbean holiday, passes out in the plane. It is the anniversary of my father's death. I'm drained and my heart is broken.


A picture in the newspaper shows a mangled wheelchair on the side of a road. Not long after this, a psychiatrist tells me that rolling into traffic is not an uncommon method of suiciding for people in wheelchairs. I read the article carefully. A man in a wheelchair is hit by a car, taken to hospital, and dies several days later. No mention of what led to the crash.

Alessandra's hospital room is a mess. There's water all over the floor. Confined to her bed due to her broken wheelchair, and frustrated, she purposely slides out. Staff want to forcibly put her back in bed in restraints. I suggest they leave her for a while on the floor. I rent a wheelchair for a week.

The following day she calls me, desperate for a nurse to change her. The pain of urine spread through her open bed sore is intolerable.

The next evening Alessandra phones from the hospital lobby to say she's leaving. After eight months there and no place else to go, she might as well leave and go to a friend's place. "Please don't leave the hospital tonight," I say. "You'll have a happy place to live. You will." I don't know what to do. If I phone her ward, they'll send security, who will be rough with her. If I don't phone, she might leave—and what then?

Alessandra feels somewhat better, no longer suicidal as she recently had been. Can she sign up for adapted skiing in the winter?

She has permission to leave the hospital grounds. Visiting a friend in his backyard, she once again struggles for breath. Her friend calls an ambulance and they go to hospital, leaving her wheelchair behind. No one from the hospital calls me.

Alessandra needs a fall jacket. Soon, she will need winter clothes and new boots.

A nurse calls at 9:30 p.m. to say that Alessandra's blood sugar levels are at a disastrous level.

The next day another nurse calls. They have just put Alessandra into restraints, she is experiencing psychosis, won't eat, won't take her meds, not even pain meds.

Her doctor phones. "She's at the highest level of drugs, antipsychotic, antidepressants, mood stabilizers. Her quality of life has gone down in the hospital. Her bed sore is not healing, and that is worrisome. She has regrets about her jump and wishes she hadn't done it. She almost set herself on fire in her room. She has overdosed several times while here, and each time it followed an interview with the transition unit, who do not admit her to a facility. She has good reasons to be angry. We aren't able to protect her while still giving her quality of life. You should explore long-term care facilities across the province and across the country."

I am aware that I need to react with calm concern, but it becomes tougher and tougher to stay balanced on that fulcrum.

Secondary traumatic stress: symptoms include isolation, unexpressed emotions, nightmares. The Compassion Fatigue Scale provides a score should the energy be available to answer the scale's questions.

November, with loss all around me, covering me. I feel unworthy, alone, a failure, perhaps I haven't accomplished anything worthwhile.

Alessandra's relationship with another staff member deteriorates. Her feet look worse, more swollen.

Long-term illness demands determination. Of sufferers as well as those who care for them. I know this, yet I feel hounded, hemmed in, stuck.

I tour a long-term care facility and leave distraught. Row on row of frail elderly residents in wheelchairs line the hallways. Staff look miserable and haggard. I'm not sure why, but I am taken to the locked basement that houses people with dementia, an even more dismal place than the hallway. Afterwards, I email my sister. *I'm reeling.*

A friend tells me she sees Alessandra on the bus quite often. "How is she doing," she asks.

Alessandra calls a friend of mine, too often. I threaten to take her phone away.

Her glasses have again been repaired. I pick them up, bring them to her. I'm discouraged. We both roil.

I overhear conversations. One young man talks to a hospital maintenance worker:

"I hear voices."

"From where?"

"Well, I don't know, but they tell me I've been bad and I'm going to be deported."

"No, you're not going to be deported."

"Oh, ok."

I set limits, mostly unsuccessful, on giving her money. Such a strong emotional valence, I'm hooked again and again. And sad, almost always.

The next time Alessandra's heart stops, she's not alone. A nurse is there. Later, she tells me Alessandra struggled to breathe, then went limp, fell back, and her eyes rolled to the back of her head. "It was lucky I was there when it occurred," the nurse says. I thank her for telling me, for being in my daughter's room when it happened.

I'm on my way to the memorial service of a friend's husband. His illness was long. My friend had over a year to prepare, if there's such a thing as preparing. During the memorial, I wonder whether I have to prepare myself for my daughter's death. *What kind of memorial service would be the best for her,* I wonder—then force myself to stop. Alessandra has survived so much. She's tough. I will die before her, and that is how it ought to be. Parents die before their children.

She teaches me to stand up for what is right, to try to fix what's wrong, to stay upright in the swirl of mental illness. I learn much about sadness. I'm proud of her courage, her capacity for acceptance, the ongoing grace with which she faces the world, lives to the fullest, refuses to give up.

I wonder what it would feel like if she didn't need me.

A friend tells me she's angry that Alessandra attempted suicide, a selfish act, she calls it. She asks why I give Alessandra money. "Just a sinkhole." I hold on.

"Try tough love," she advises. "Issue consequences. Just sit her down, and tell her your expectations."

"The circle is getting tighter," says another friend. "It's closing in on her, isn't it?"

I don't respond.

Did she assume I'd find this helpful? Or, and this is hard—am I angry, do I think she's gone too far and is wrong besides, because I don't want to face the truth? Fear and disbelief jostle in me, side by side.

Casual remarks about mental illness—from a friend, a professional, or a stranger expecting agreement—can knock me off balance.

*A nut case, she's mental, crazy, she's all fucked up. He's in woowoo land all right. She looks like she just walked out of a looney bin. He should be locked up. Give her a lobotomy. Lunatic. He needs his head read. Belongs in the mental, the funny farm, the nut house. She's on a broom stick, flying over the cuckoo's nest.*

Or any variation of *that murderer must have been deranged to have done that, no one in their right mind would do that,* criminality conflating with mental illness.

How to capture the right tone, respond cogently. My brain totters, stumbles. My unease tests my desperation to protect my daughter.

A police officer is under investigation for allegedly filming himself mocking women with mental health issues. The videos are said to show him mocking and ridiculing these women whom he arrested or apprehended under the Mental Health Act. Those videos, allegedly filmed by him while in the driver's seat of his cruiser with the women in the backseat, were then circulated among other police officers for them to watch.

I need equilibrium. Instead, my anger escalates.

I struggle to take care of my needs, show an interest in social activities, keep my family from toppling.

I do my best to hang on amidst the chaos and ill health; maintain a positive perspective; keep balance no matter what. I succeed less often now. I want to influence decision-makers to do the right thing, to make things right. But often I'm in freefall, or depressed, or deep in grief for my daughter's accumulating losses.

How to answer *what are your daughter's interests?*

What about *her health* or *a mind free of pain?*

How to answer *how are you?*
*Fine* is the easy answer. *Drained, completely.*

How do you take care of yourself? *Get through one day, get through the next, then the next.*

Alessandra phones saying she feels like she's in a dream. Food tastes bad. She's angry. Again, she says, "My legs are no good, what good am I?" Later that day, I unplug my phone because she won't stop calling. She wants to get out of there, leave tonight. How can I maintain compassion?

How can I maintain my own sanity?

Her doctor. "Alessandra's physical health is not good. Her diabetes is out of control. Her blood sugar levels are skyrocketing. It's catching up with her, her legs and her vision will be affected, and she will need dialysis, she will lose a leg and she will be blind. Her kidney is large, compensating for having only one. During the past three months, she has been in the intensive care unit several times. She has recently had a chest x-ray, abdominal ultrasound, a blood infection, her kidney has been checked out. Her foot was broken. Her wrists were damaged. She was put into restraints. She's lost a lot and won't regain most of it, and eating is one of her few pleasures. She's lethargic and drowsy. She's desperate to have a home."

# Home

## Last weeks of

So begins the dark month, November

How do I not give in to despair? Again and again, I shore myself up by clinging to hopes the size now of molecules. Our emotions clang against each other more persistently, and my worry wildly intensifies to panic. I am desperate to keep her alive. Never believing that she, whose spirit is so big, she, who several times has been only seconds from death, would die. I now approach each day with trepidation.

A friend cries during a phone call. "Can't you do more to find a home for Alessandra?"

I attend a meeting about another possible housing placement. No result. This place can't provide for her physical health needs. And I'm told most residents use crack cocaine. Alessandra has never succumbed to illegal drugs, but would she be tempted in a situation like that?

Alessandra disowns me for two days.

Again, I'm overwhelmed by restlessness, isolation, and nightmares in which someone is about to kill me. Shame and depression are winning. Will life smooth out? I think about my mother. Shy, like me, an introvert. Her younger brother, George, was ill from his early twenties until he died in his early thirties. Did she care for him? Did it make her protective? Did she feel regret? I wonder now, too late, why I never asked.

Getting through by shutting down, cutting off. A shadow stays beside me, always there somehow, following from one horror to another.

Mental illness hurts the heart.

# Home

## Empty

On the sea of the heavens

Waves of cloud arise,

The moon-a boat-

Amongst a forest of stars

Rows on, hidden, or so it seems.

—Kakinomoto no Hitomaro

# PART II

**Obituary**. Alessandra Arleen Sharkey passed away November 16, 2013 while in hospital. She participated in life with a huge and happy spirit. Never shy, she had many friends and was able to bring much joy into the lives of a wide range of people. She was a member of Propeller Dance and participated in several of the troupe's annual performances. She sang beautifully, possessing a voice with depth and strength, comparable to the voice of singer, Nina Simone. She has left an enormous hole in the world that no one, nothing can replace. She will be missed terribly.

Her death had not appeared imminent to me.

The state of shock on hearing these words—psychosis, overdose, suicide attempt, razor blade across the wrist, homeless shelter, another shelter, then another, another suicide attempt, another, then another.

But then the word dead—the state of desolation, longing.

# Home

## Parable of

A woman whose child had died asked Siddhartha to bring the child back to life. Siddhartha said: Go to every house in the village and bring me back a pinch of white mustard seed from any where there has never been a death. If you return with the mustard seed, I will bring your child back to life.

The woman went to all the homes. She did not return to the Buddha.

# The Mother

When the mother wakes up in the morning, she fumbles to slump through time, to organize her life, to get through to the other side of shock. Caregiving has torn apart her own mental health.

To talk about death is one thing, but how to talk about her own child's death without the child getting lost in the telling? The story of exhaustion, frustration, terror. How to convey the child, simply the child?

The past world sticks to her. The mother needs to pulls memories out from where they're stuck. Not knowing what else to do with the crowding memories, she begins to write a journal. Will writing deliver her? Release her?

It is one thing, often commendable, to reveal your true self in public. It is something else again to reveal another person's life. Especially when that person isn't there to speak for herself. I'm doing that.

The mother's guilt.

The mother stands as the fulcrum between her own mother and her daughter. The mother grew up pulled towards shame, even so, she never imagined that becoming a parent would steep her in that feeling. Always wanting to fit in. Never fitting in. Trying to pass. Not passing.

Now she wants to let go of the silence, self-judgment, and secrecy. Now she wants to release the shame.

What rises then is anger. Anger for allowing shame to rule her; shame for bottling her anger, pushing it down. Anger and shame, shame and anger, in a toxic, too familiar brew.

How could she not have known? Her daughter's heart had stopped several times. Even that afternoon, it had stopped. Had she been protecting herself, lying to herself, while the possibility—no, the probability—lay deep in her unconscious? Why had she cut out an ad for a new funeral cooperative and kept it on her desk? Why was it not obvious? Or was it?

She should have known that she had been already in mourning for a long time: mourning her daughter's broken potential; mourning her early trauma, the shattering. Mourning her daughter's energetic self— no longer bicycling, rollerblading, leaping to dunk a basketball, running with her dog.

Mourning that her daughter would never wear a police officer's badge; mourning her brain damaged as a result of a suicide attempt and her spine fractured from another; that she would never bring her personal items into a permanent home, remaining warehoused; mourning the scant attention to her cardiac arrests leaving her minutes, maybe seconds from death; always mourning.

The mother grieves for her daughter's losses.

She feels guilty that she could not allow herself to know that death was coming.

Often, strangers stopped Alessandra on the street, at a bus stop, in a coffee shop. "Why are you in a wheelchair?" Alessandra answered, politely. She was kind, present in the moment to others, even as strangers stared, or looked away fast, or looked through her.

Guilt and grief and indebtedness conjoin when the mother thinks of how her own world expanded because her daughter's energy and kindness and presence touched others in precious ways. Because of this showing, the mother's world expanded. This was the daughter's gift to the mother. Is death the price her daughter had to pay for the giving?


The mother's swirling jumble of emotions, the fits of boiling anger. The mother desperate to protect her daughter, anxious where her daughter's vulnerability might lead, where her trust could carry. The bubbling of mother love.

The mother felt many things about the daughter—among them, love, irritation, exhaustion, protection—and through it all maintained a loyalty to her daughter's spirit and a hope embodied in their shared laughter over puns, enjoyment of meals together, solving puzzles by the fireplace, hiking in nature. Meanwhile, the daughter, like her mother, felt—must have felt—anger and disappointment, but never lost her loyalty to those she loved, would stand beside them, stand up for them.

Like her mother, the daughter's emotions churned—yet she remained loyal. Sometimes her daughter's mind didn't hold still. Sometimes her daughter argued with her oldest friend, Helen, but then the friendship discontinued. All the time, her daughter was faithful to those close, all the time she loved, protected her younger sister, her mother, her dog, but not enough herself.

The mother is falling in one direction, toward depression. How to face this. *She goes to bed. She gets out of bed.* The task of getting up to make a cup of coffee.

She stands in for many others, the linked, ongoing witnesses.

Her home is different now.

Still her failure

to keep her daughter alive. She didn't do that. After she first met her daughter, she signed the adoption papers and two days later brought her daughter home. A permanent contract. No turning back. Wrestling to provide ease, a vision of a less tumultuous future, reasons to stay alive, wrestling for physical health care, psychiatric care, housing, at times any housing, wrestling with herself for energy, wisdom, the right tone to speak, grappling to inch open the systems' thick gates, wrestling with love to cure.

Her failure sits on her shoulders like concrete.

# Home

## If only

For years I had been keeping my phone beside my bed at night. Just in case.

Emergencies had happened.

One more emergency.

From her

*I'm in emergency. Please come.*

From a hospital

*She's here. She's not doing well. In intensive care. Come.*

I knew there would be other emergencies, knew another call would come, but the shock when the phone rang in the night, the night after I didn't meet Alessandra for breakfast.

I should have known.

I shoot out of sleep to standing in what feels like one motion. The phone sharp as a fire alarm. 3:30 a.m. The nurse's voice is calm. "Alessandra had a great morning, her day was spent at a friend's place, and she was cheery in the evening back at the hospital."

As I listen, I know, I just know, and I want to push her to get to the point. Do they all give a long introduction? Are they taught to do this? Don't they know this causes a person to want to scream. *What is it, tell me what's wrong?*

The nurse went to Alessandra's room at 2:00 a.m. and Alessandra was breathing well. When she returned at 2:30 a.m., my daughter wasn't breathing.

"Wasn't breathing," I yell. "Is she dead?"

"Code blue, they 'worked on her' for thirty-five minutes. It was unexpected. Get a glass of water and drink a sip. Wait till morning to come to the hospital. We will keep her body in her bed until you've come."

"Her body," I scream, "What about her?"

The switch from present to past tense comes so quickly. 'She' becomes 'the body.' Just like that.

We hang up.

I pace. Hard. The heels of my bare feet hammer the floor as I pitch from one end of the room to the other. *What do I do, what do I do?* I say it again and again, hear myself saying it.

Then, I sob.

I walk through every room in the house, I keep walking. I go to the kitchen and make a cup of tea, turn on my computer, and check emails. After a few minutes I think, what am I doing? I don't know why I'm checking emails, what do I hope to find? An email saying my daughter's alive?

I have to phone someone. In the middle of the night. Wake up someone to say my daughter is dead. I phone a friend in another province. Maybe she will know what to do, how to solve this problem, maybe she will tell me my daughter is really alive.

But instead, she says, "Phone Jane, she'll go with you to the hospital."

I say, "No it's the middle of the night. I'll go on my own."

But I know I can't, and I phone Jane. I try to get dressed, taking clothes out of my closet and throwing them one by one on to the floor, not knowing what to put on.

I phone my friend back. "I can't get dressed." She tells me to put on jeans and a sweater. I get dressed.

The intubation equipment is still in my daughter's mouth and held in place by white tape around her cheeks. Her face is to the side, as though looking out the window of her room, but her eyes are closed. The resuscitation equipment stands close to her bed. The read-out of her heart, the flat-line proving it wasn't pumping, on the table. The floor of her room strewn with bits of plastic wrappings torn from equipment to save lives.

We stay for an hour, a lifetime's journey with her. Still dark outside.

The first time I met Renata was in the orphanage when I went there to bring Alessandra home. Renata had been transferred to that orphanage just three months earlier. It would be another year and a half before she could join our family, rejoin her sister. A long wait. Renata and I often talk about when she was four years old and first came to Canada.

Now, I'm waiting to tell her that her sister is dead.

The morning after Alessandra's death, Renata is returning from a holiday. I wait until she arrives home. At noon, she bounces happily into the house. "I had such a great time!"

Then she sees my face.

"What's wrong?"

I lead her upstairs to my bedroom and I say the words. She stares at me. Stands up. Stands still. Then come questions. We cry. She paces, she sits down and we hold each other, wiping away tears.

"Oh Mum, poor you, I'm so sorry for you."

We stay beside each other on the edge of the bed. I'm so sorry for her.

I take her to the hospital. Her sister still lies in her room. It's afternoon and a lot is happening on the unit. People mill around, chatting, playing board games, watching TV. Someone talks loudly on a phone.

We walk through the ward to Alessandra's room, arm in arm, taking slow, careful steps. The tile floor wobbles. The walls float toward me then away. That this is the last time I will see my daughter. The awareness makes my breathing rough, haggard.

Renata opens the door to Alessandra's room and walks in first. Away from the clamour of the ward, the room stuns with a brittle silence. Renata whispers something to me, then moves towards her sister. She strokes her sister's head, gently kisses her forehead.

"Oh, Alessandra."

We want to stay, not sure how to leave. How to go to the door, open it, and walk away?

Never to hear her voice, or see her smile. Never to visit, to joke with her, to share small habits, to hug each other?

How can I walk away and into a life without her?

But I do open the door. I stop, look back, and whisper.

"Goodbye, Alessandra."

Then the hall. How to walk along the hallway towards the exit on the wobbling floor, my eyes flitting, the walls blurring, floating. Slow motion.

Half way to the exit, I hear a patient call us. I stop and she holds out a pair of red shoes.

"I want Alessandra to have these. Last night she told me she liked them, so I want her to have them."

"Thank you," Renata replies. "But why don't you keep them. She won't be wearing them."

At the front desk, a nurse points to three garbage bags containing Alessandra's clothes and belongings. We take them.

Renata and I leave the hospital, leave Alessandra, leave life as I know it.

Her clothes, a ring, a watch, glasses, books. We carry her belongings home. When I open her wallet, it contains $6.10. Her money. All of it. I keep it on my bureau for four months.

# Lacrimation

The word is distinguished, hushed. It rings so gently, so nobly on the inner ear.

And Jesus, just like us. *Lacrima Christi.*

But tears are not gracious. They are jarring, hard to control, impossible to hide. Undignified. Public.

The first day, my tears leave salt lines that stick and penetrate like pin pricks into my cheeks, my chin.

On the second day, my sinuses hurt.

After three days, the muscles of my face ache, my jaw feels as though I've been punched.

By the fourth day, fingertips burn like sandpaper against the delicate skin below my eyes.

On the fifth day, my nose bloats like a dead fish come to shore. I lean to one side to drain a nostril. Ultrasoft tissues scrape across my face like nails.

Salt digs into pore after pore, pushing its way deeper, like burrowing insects, micro-spears piercing the skin. Raw blotches of dry skin redden my cheeks. Creams sting like lit matches.

The accumulation of salt, the power of salt. I'm turning to salt.

My shoulders slump. Head seems heavy for my body. Neck tired. Feet swollen. My face breaks out with acne. Many cups of tea are offered, and I accept each cup and drink from each one offered. My stomach swells with tea. Tannin stands for love and care.

After the memorial, I won't drink tea for four months.

I don't know how to believe that my daughter is dead, so I say to myself, *It's hard to believe.*

As if saying that might produce belief.

Maybe she will visit, or maybe she'll phone and say, *Let's go out for breakfast!* And we'll decide what time we'll meet at Rockin' Johnny's.


Painful to think about her, painful not to. I try to push thoughts of her away, yet need to feel her up close beside me. My bones taut for wanting to hold, to hug.


At my daughter's memorial, they say

*definitely I'll be in touch with you ... I'll see you in a month ... I'll email you, soon ... we'll have lunch for sure ... I'll contact you ... I'll remember I promise ... I'll call ... yes, definitely ... some time next month*

Later, they may have thought

*I don't know what I'd talk about ... it would be awkward ... and who wants that ... you know I don't really know her that well ... besides, I don't want to disturb her ... anyway she must be over it by now ... life goes on, you know ... I forgot to call, been so busy recently ... a month, that's long enough isn't it ... I'm really busy ... she probably wouldn't want me to call ... my work's crazy ... it would be a downer for me   busy ... another time, later ... she must be fine ... I would be anyway*

# Home

## Three weeks


I hear about death cafés, death games, courses, memorials that celebrate, laugh, cheer, refuse mourning. But this,

this

> tangle of grief, depression, burnout, all roped together. How long until the loosening and untangling? And then to what? Crumpled, I want to run away. The isolation of loss. I find myself afraid of blanking out, afraid of elevators, of getting stuck in one, dying in one.

It's evening and I'm bereft, missing her. Shame, ever my companion, chides me still.

*You should be stronger. You should rise above it, wash your kitchen floor. You should rest. You shouldn't avoid people, you should have a dinner party, let people in. You should keep people safe from your negativity. You should put on a brave face. You should know how to save yourself. You should get some help.*

*You shouldn't let yourself get sunk in grief, you are wrong for doing that. Your grief is a cause for shame.*

I berate myself for that.

For years, it seemed my caregiving duties kept me pinned down. But now, instead of relief, I feel stuck. I feel the tug of time. I want to appear less pathetic than I feel. I regret that I was impatient with her when I saw her the last time. I was grumpy. I made lunch for her, shared quirky stories, but I could have been cheerier.

She had beaten so many odds that it seemed she wore a suit of armour, and chinks in her armour were just that.

Her childhood letters to me predicting an early death

her deep depressions
a noose found hanging from an exposed beam in the basement
that time she drank gasoline . . .
early chinks in her protective armour?


Then

the times she swallowed too many pills
cut her wrist
fell hard on harder pavement. . .
more chinks in her armour?

Cardiac arrest
three months later, again
a month after that
the morning before
but I avoided knowledge, limping forward.
I never believed.


People tell me Alessandra will live forever in my heart. What is that heart of which they speak? That tennis ball muscle so near exploding, still pounding with shock, its arteries frayed beyond patching?

Or is it a word for memory?

And my daughter, who started life in whose arms, did she pass a happy time close to that first other heart, tucked in, floating fearlessly, inquisitively? Swimming mightily, perhaps Olympian in the amniotic, how did she move from one contained world to another? Was it hard to leave that cosmos of fullness, to come to air? Heart touching heart through skin, beat by beat, her heart close to whose bigger heart?

Alessandra's heart, beat by beat, leaning into a bigger heart. That bigger heart, does it still beat in memory of the two hearts, beat in the missing of the other heart?

Now past this air world, past us, perhaps past her first heart-close, to where hearts don't beat, don't hurt, don't near-explode. My heart close to exploding, holding back a tsunami of pain in this hardly real life. Beats missing, heart pounding hard for three.

In the parsing of a life some people say, *Give it a couple of months.* Some say, *Give it a year. Then you'll be over it.*

Some friends say

*Alessandra's organs were closing down.*

Although that is not true.

*Her death is a relief. Her body and her lively spirit didn't match each other. She was too lively for her body.*

*Be strong.*

*I can't console you. Nothing I would say will console you, so I won't say anything.*

*I believe in reincarnation, so it's not forever.*

*This world is made for us to suffer.*

Other friends say

*You should have known she was dying.*

*Are you avoiding me?*

*Do you feel guilty? I hear that most parents do when their child dies.*

*I have no reference point. How do I respond with no reference point?*

*I went to a bereavement group when my father died. You should go.*

*She's finally free.*

*I have to ask you a question. Why are you grieving?*

Acquaintances say

*I understand. My son might go away to university next year. I rely on him, so I don't want him to get accepted. We should go for coffee some time. I'm looking to make a friend.*

*I know what it's like, it's just like love. Grief and love are the same, they're intense emotions and feel the same, so I know how you feel. I've been in love.*

*You only get what you can handle.*

It's not all like that. People say thoughtful things, too many to mention. But the hard things stick in my heart.

Alessandra's ashes are tucked into a box on the mantle and Renata places a piece of lush pink quartz on top. I add Alessandra's friendship ring and a key chain she made in the hospital.

A longstanding plan to visit an out-of-town friend had been scheduled for what turns out to be three weeks after Alessandra's death. My friend encourages me to come, but it's not possible to put clothes into a suitcase, let alone to leave Alessandra and act like a proper guest. I text my friend a message and receive a terse reply.

I should be able to visit.

Nothing feels right.

Backing out of my driveway, I stop for an ambulance parked at the next house. A neighbour rushes towards me, puts her head into my car's side window.

"Another one bites the dust, ha."

I stare at her. She knew my daughter, saw her just a month ago.

She stands up.

"Oh," she says. "Sorry."

In the dentist's office, I'm captive and silenced—my eyes closed, my mouth full of gauze. The dental assistant details her eighteen-year-old niece's death from a rare illness. How the illness progressively worsened, how the parents of the girl felt, and how coping is so difficult for them even now, three years on.

My feet are in the mud of it. How far from ordinary am I?

Rewind. Apologize for the tears. I made someone see me cry. That person piled up her courage to look at me, to say the words, not to run off somewhere, and this is what I give her, tears.

I'm socially inadequate, my mind foggy, and one more time, I excuse myself from attending a social event. What can I add to any discussion? The weather? Politics? Culture, the arts, sports? I blank on all of these.

And if asked, *How's life?* or *What do you do?* How would I answer?

**Old search histories**

international adoption

sexual and physical abuse of children

ADHD

self-harm

learning disabilities

traumatic brain injury

mental illness

systems—psychiatric, social services, prison

homelessness

life in institutions

facilities

paraplegia

sarcoidosis

diabetes

arthritis

pressure sores

human warehousing.


**Now I look up**

bereaved parenthood

I continue to unravel. I lack confidence, feel tentative, unreal. Everywhere, I see danger. I imagine earthquakes, lightning strikes, and house fires in an unpredictable and tilted world, a place where unravelling occurs. My surroundings appear different and I don't recognize myself.

I'm not in the world of the ordinary person, I've moved over the line, into an empty space. Am I like an alien to others?

Now an anxious driver, I'm afraid I'll sideswipe another car, fail to spot a pedestrian in front of me. My reactions become sluggish, so I devise tactics: avoid highways; grip the steering wheel tight. As though gripping will keep me safe.

I'm small.

When people ask me how I cope, I have no answer. "I'm so sorry," they say, and I nod. But I feel it in how they touch my arm and the feeling surrounds me. When I look up, I see what they're thinking. *I'm glad it wasn't me, but it could never be me. Things like that don't happen to me.* I see them rush away from the abysmal thought that it could happen to them.

I sleep fitfully and in short chapters, waking up in the night with my solar plexus taut, as though in combat. On edge, odd thoughts bounce around my brain as it zips through to questions demanding attention but with no clear answers. *Where are the dead, where is my daughter? Am I supposed to feel her presence? If I don't, what does that say—about me, about life, about death?*

*What does it mean to have meaning?*

My father had a large horseshoe tattoo on his right inner forearm. When I was ten, it fascinated me, though even then, it was already fading, and since then, I haven't thought about it in years. Now, inexplicably I want a tattoo just like his. But I never go to get it, because planning for it feels too daunting.

Restless, I wake up one night and go to my window. Snow falls, the scene idyllic, a sign of the world moving, while I remain stuck. I watch the night snow tumble down from its dark source like tears down a face.

How to contain grief.

Lured by the safety of my bed, I let it become a raft, although it fails to save me. I fear losing composure, fear losing my sanity. I fight against remaining stuck. *Get up, move!* I need to release the pent energy tightening my chest, head, jaw. Something pushing to the surface, needing to be grappled. I imagine that this is how an addict feels, this tension.

I have no schedule. Routines, I see, can be a succor and must keep so many from going over the edge. Garbage day is how I organize my life. Each Thursday rolls around and tells me another week has passed.

> Takotsubo cardiomyopathy, broken heart syndrome, is a weakening of the left ventricle, the heart's main pumping chamber. It disrupts the normal pumping function of the heart. Common symptoms are chest pain and shortness of breath.

# Christmas

## Another

Alessandra died in November. Five weeks away from Christmas. As the season closes in, I have no desire to decorate, no taste to celebrate. At the last moment, my plan to ignore the day having grown more painful than not, I invite two friends for dinner with Renata and me. One friend's dog becomes the day's therapy animal. My other friend joins us with her kitten. And the day, a hurdle, is done. One hurdle of many.

# Boxing Day

Having survived Christmas, I expect the next day to be easier, but I'm wrong, and on Boxing Day, I fall into myself.

*It doesn't make sense, I don't understand, I want her back.*

Mostly I say, *Why don't I feel her presence?*

Not yet knowing the cause of her death, I imagine it might have been prevented, but could it?

Her friend Kevin drops by to pick up a laptop I no longer use. He tells me that he and Alessandra had planned to go to a mall the morning after her death. That morning, when he arrived at her ward, a nurse told him that she died in the night. He turned and left. After sitting for a while on a bench outside the hospital, he got on a bus and returned to his room. He leaves my place with the laptop, containers of leftover Christmas dinner, and a plasticized copy of Alessandra's obituary. He will place it neatly on a table in his room.

Back in my house, I look out the living room window to the wheelchair ramp. The last time I saw her, she had just come down that ramp. As I backed up the car so she could get past the driveway, she was smiling and waving to me. "Bye mum, I love you." Kevin, steadfast, walked behind her. I watched as they rounded the corner, hurrying to catch a bus.

The following day I determine to strike a balance and I go on my own to a play, a desperately sad story about a boy marked by unfathomable misfortunes and heartbreaks. A bad choice, I apprehend, minutes after the first act begins, and I cry softly through most of it. Afterwards, I dash to the privacy of my car, where I wail in the dark for the boy, for my daughter, for her challenges, her endurance, her losses. Like the boy in that play, she carried on, so optimistically life-loving, except when living felt unimaginable.

# Home

## New year

Did I mention that Alessandra loved our fireplace? We often sat in front of it, watching the flames, feeling its heat, once in a while talking. Being there together brought us mutual calm, so these were cherished times. The New Year's Eve before her death, we'd sat cozy and contented with prosecco, brie, crackers, thin slices of carrot cake, in the glow of those flames.

"I want to take care of you when you're old," she said. She'd often said this. And having graduated from college with a certificate to work with the elderly, she felt she would know what to do.

So many times, even as a young girl, she would say this.

"But how can I now, so difficult to do that in a wheelchair."

Later that evening, the New Year's Eve before she died, she fell asleep in front of the fire, a duvet tucked up to her chin. I read a mystery on the couch beside her. At nearly midnight, leftover cake in hand to give to the staff, she called out, "Happy New Year, I love you, Mum," as she was guided into an accessible cab for her return journey to hospital.

A good omen, a start I believed that would bring improvements to health as well as a turnaround to her desperate housing situation.

That night, I slept satisfied.

This New Year's Eve, I don't want to walk into a new year. I stare at a wall in my living room. I feel the lonesomeness of death, the sensation of separateness, how it clogs my ability to connect.

This year, this new year coming six weeks after Alessandra's death, this year I don't want, this year that will begin many years without her, arrives with a dank sky overhead. All the same, I cling to some hope that the first of the month, in its newness, will bring some small comfort, perhaps some dissipation of grief.

This doesn't happen. I feel morose, worn out. I don't see Renata that day, and although we had made no plan, I desperately want to see her, prepare a special meal to fight through my gloom. Instead I eat fried eggs, telling myself as I eat to sit up straight. Nagging myself to shift from the slump I have acquired in the past six weeks.

Because

posture matters in my fight for my emotional life. If I sit up straight, as the nuns in my childhood insisted, if I do things right, if I act like a proper girl, a proper woman, a proper mother, will she come back?

If I go out of the house, especially if I go far, I could miss her. I can't go far, just in case she comes home.

It's ridiculous to think she'll ring my doorbell, and I know this, but if I accept that this will never happen, I might implode. She might, she really might show up, just as she'd done so many times before. This secret thought holds me together. I rarely leave my house. I am almost a shut-in.

Am I agoraphobic? How would I know?

But by mid-January, I have to get away. Far away. I have to leave the madness of my mind, even though that means leaving Alessandra.

I spend six days with my sister and her partner, Chris, on the west coast, away from the home where Alessandra grew up. I stand out of time for six days. Anxious. Mostly in a daze. Still.

Back in my own house, I'm edgier, wanting even more to be away. With two friends, I fly south, spending afternoons in bed, sometimes reading, at other times staring at a wall.

Late one day, as the sun sets over the ocean, I walk along the empty beach, following the undulating line where water and sand come together, move away and come together again, the line where nothing is definite. Alone, I call into the horizon over the waves.

"Alessandra, I'm here, be here with me. Where are you?"

My voice loud, powerful, so full of desire. Its drum-like sound startles me as I call her again and again, her name rolling over the ocean. *Alessandra, Alessandra.*

Back home, I become culpable. Phone calls remain unanswered. Friends invite me for dinners, but I can't commit. People leave messages but their emails just clutter my inbox. I've separated myself from the world, and taking an ordinary step or moving sideways, I fear I might fall.

Heavy waves of grief.

On a February afternoon, I spend three hours stuck. My brain feels like many cars circling into the centre, all poised toward the same midpoint until they crash against each other, impossible for any to release, to move. How to get unstuck?

As a young girl, I read every Nancy Drew mystery. I loved her courage, the way she'd venture into basements, attics, and abandoned houses to solve mysteries, to make the world right. A friend who spends hours at her dining room table putting puzzle pieces together, ordering the world, gives me a thousand-piece Nancy Drew puzzle. "You'll love it," she tells me.

I follow her instructions: lay out the pieces in front of me on a table; look carefully at the picture; find the pieces for the margins first; enjoy.

But my mind jumps around too much. For weeks, the pieces lie across my table. Every day, I return to try the assemblage, hoping to succeed at this small task. But I fail, and fail again, and when I can no longer face this failure, I put the pieces back into their box.

Driving through a quiet neighbourhood, I notice a young woman on the sidewalk looking directly at me. Astonished, I realize it's Alessandra. *She's here!* I speed around the block and return to the spot, now empty. Then I remember how a month after my mother died, I saw her, walking in front of me on a street in Montréal, wearing her favourite beige dress. I saw my father too, shortly after his death, on a street in another city, sporting his pork pie hat, whistling as he often did.

I yearn to read grief. Perhaps this will be my way to clarity, to comprehend death, to find a touchstone in my aloneness. Some people dash off to an ashram or rush into marriage, some shut down and can't talk about what has happened, others talk about it a lot, some can't read anything, not a recipe, not a pamphlet. And some, like me, are compelled to read.

I read how-to books by experts on getting over grief, memoirs predominantly by wives describing their husbands' deaths, their guidelines for moving on. Few books describe the death of a child. For hours each day I read, often crying as I do, and sometimes unexpectedly, I sob. My craving for these books continues.

# Home

## Three months

Fretting, I attempt to establish some minimal order. My home needs cleaning, past-dated food needs to be tossed. I speculate whether doing is superior to being; doing, that judgment of worth, one's value to the world. I stand on unsteady ground with that notion and count the days since my life turned. I wonder, is the pain on my face visible?

Over this time, my grief shifts. Moves to different parts of the body. A constant headache calls out for relief. My back tightens. I'm drawn in, round shouldered. I feel uncomfortably curled up, stooped. Grief shapes my body as well as my interior life, makes me a stranger to my former self.

# Home

## Sometimes out

Near the exit of a corner store, I become aware of a woman who looks a lot like Alessandra. I pass her, pause and wait for her, but she doesn't move. I turn and ask if she wants to walk with me. We walk slowly, but we don't talk. When we are out of the store and down a block, she turns and I watch her. After a few steps, she stops again. I suggest again that we walk together. After a few minutes she says, "I'm all right now. I can go on my own."

At the check-out counter of another store the elderly man ahead of me moves sadly, bewilderedly, his expression an admission of hard circumstance. I greet him. "Hello." Surprised, his answer is serious, curt. Leaving the store, he moves slowly down the street. I recognize this gait. It is oddly familiar.

I worry that others will tell me to buck up. Maybe I should buck up, although I don't know how.

A heart can be constricted. A heart can crack wide-open and never be the same again.

Cards from Alessandra's memorial stay in an envelope, unread. I overeat, preferring comfort food. Colours elude me and interactions with people drain. My chest remains tight, my breathing thin, my body heavy. Aspirin salves a dull, low throbbing headache. Unshifting, sadness stays stuck. My shrunken world holds small, keeps me fearful.

With a sudden sharp pang, I realize that Alessandra truly is not coming back. She slips farther and farther away. In the sameness of each morning, I feel old, my hands reminding me of my grandmother's. My periods of numb turmoil, the hours I lay on my couch in what kind of state is it anyway? I say to my sister, "When am I going to get going?" and for some reason, it sounds funny, and we both burst out laughing. But still I'm stuck.

Each day is a struggle for a neighbour who suffers from mental illness. She knocks on my door with a Black angel figurine. "Alessandra had a hard life and terrible illness. I wouldn't wish it on anyone." I put the angel beside the urn on the mantle.

A friend brings dinner to my place. How did she know?

I hear about how others cope.

How this person felt when a parent or grandparent died. How that person felt when he lost a spouse. I accumulate a collection of these stories. People, it seems, long for permission to talk about death, to relate meaning.

I meet someone who, following the death of his son, wrote numerous letters to him, writing his grief to his son.

And someone else, whose son died five years earlier at the age of twenty-five, rails against those who expect him to get over it.

I question a friend whose daughter died eight years before. What does time do, I want to know.

"Holidays and celebrations are like sawdust."

I talk with a man whose son died by suicide. He tells me he does not know how he can go on. Startled, I assume he means that he would like to kill himself. Then I understand. He doesn't know how to move out of wrenching grief, past never doing, not accomplishing.

An acquaintance tells me that her brother died when he was twenty years old, and watching the pain of her parents was unbearable.

Sophia Tolstoy, wife of the famous novelist Leo and mother of thirteen, lost five of them as children. "There is nothing as painful and dreadful as a mother's grief at the loss of her child," she said.

A grief she suffered five times over.

And my mother's mother suffered that way three times.


The lonely period extends. Friends stop asking me how I'm doing, stop mentioning my daughter. They assume, or want to assume, that I'm over it.

But my mind remains indolent, my muscles ache. Walking upstairs hurts. I cry at films, at other people's stories, at a radio show on organ transplants, on reading a gift card. Stumbling along through the gloom of this strange land, how can I get back to the living?


No easy escape. Grief insists that I do the time.


Friends no longer ask, "How are your daughters?" Now they say, "How is your daughter."

And the fraught question, "How many children do you have?"

I have to practice the words so that when I say them, they don't sound rehearsed, so that I don't break down.

This is how. First pause, think it through, then speak. Hesitate after a few sentences to gather thoughts. Conclude with a final summative sentence. Let the refrain of my rehearsal play inside my head. *Thank you, little brain, you did it. Thank you, little heart, you withstood it.* While I add, out loud, "And what about you? Tell me about your work."

The first time I'm asked the question I splutter something, but the words come out.

The next time a friend, toughened by exigencies of a nursing career, answers for me. "She has two daughters. One died three months ago. One lives here in the city."

And that's it. The questioner nods. The conversation shifts to her home renovation plans. I hold on.

# Home

## More going out of

I want endorphins, but at my infrequently attended aerobics classes, my feet move as though through quicksand, almost stuck in it, almost too slow to follow. When the song "Leaving on a Jet Plane" is played I'm caught off guard. Grief springs without warning and physical exertion and emotional plodding collide. I want to curl up in a ball.

A woman in the class often goes out of her way to ask me how I'm doing. She asks me to go for coffee with her some time. We never do, but my appreciation remains. Another classmate tells me her twenty-four-year-old son died nine years ago. When we meet in a coffee shop, she leans toward me. "I've come to realize that his life was hard and maybe it was a blessing that he died. He was always struggling." She gives me advice: dress well, put on jewellery every day, volunteer, and make yourself go to exercise class. But I love t-shirts and jeans, rarely wear jewellery, I don't have energy to volunteer, although I do try to attend exercise class.

She tells me she can't empathize when she hears of horrific tragedies. "It's how it is," she confides in a barely audible voice. "I'm dead inside."

My mind leaps to Alessandra, who lived with a dead kidney inside of her following a suicide attempt. Her broken left hip, a result of the same attempt, also never fixed. *She doesn't have feeling. It won't matter,* I was told. It did and caused ongoing pain. Death and life co-existing, entwined. Layers of death.

Leaving the coffee shop, I pass a woman wearing a sparkling Santa brooch on her coat. Alessandra would have loved it, she would have told the woman so, and she would have worn a Santa brooch if she had had one.

With no warning, I'm sabotaged as I open the door to the cold air.

I register to join a ten-week bereavement group for parents whose child has died, and at the first session, wanting to bolt, I take the seat nearest the door. The facilitators appear calm. I look at each of the other parents and they look back at me, awkwardly. Each of us shares stories of our child's death and these stories comfort the community that begins to form. One of the facilitators tells us:

"Take time each day to grieve." Easy.

"Be kind to yourself." Not so easy.

"Help others understand grief." Hard.

"Drive home carefully." I get myself home.

Not easy to talk except at this grief support group, where everyone, like me, is desperate to understand, to heal. Our feelings and thoughts are knotted together, we are all that much alike. All of us on a train rumbling past life.

I possess just enough emotional strength to get to each meeting. After each one, I spend two days drained, but I start to look forward to going to the meetings. Each of us brings three items that belonged to our child. The items I choose, so intimately connected with my daughter that I feel exposed, my privacy unveiled.

A friend emails me wanting to know about the meeting. I reply

*How consoling it was, the stories of the relationships between the children and their parents, no sugar coating. The poignancy as each item was passed around. Photos, jewellery, a son's t-shirt—everyone touching the objects of special meaning, seeing the faces of the children in their pictures, up close, in the world. I brought the picture of my daughter you suggested, standing in a forest, both arms outstretched, a bird in each of her hands. She looks in awe of the world, in prayer to nature.*

Like stones on the chest, grief hurts the breathing, challenges the moving forward.

*A famous writer's husband has dementia. She's the caretaker*

*A fifty-year-old woman is found hanging in her basement*

*A young father of three dies tragically*

*After a car accident a bank executive with a head injury can't do up his shoes, can't count*

*A twenty-one-year-old woman overdoses on crack cocaine. She is found dead with a needle in her arm*

*A fifteen-year-old gay boy shoots himself through the mouth*

*A mother is murdered*

*Someone's eighteen-year-old son acts strangely, the family learns he has schizophrenia*

*My friend, a single mother whose daughter is nine, dies slowly from an uncommon cancer*

*Another friend has cancer*

*Another friend has cancer*

*Another friend has cancer*

# Home

## Renata at

January. I'm apprehensive that Renata might unexpectedly die and wonder whether she thinks that about me. Do we both want to take care of each other? I tell her, "I miss Alessandra," and she tells me that she thinks about her sister every day.

"It's so much quieter, isn't it?"

At work, a newly hired colleague asked her about siblings, and she found herself crying.

She is looking to buy a house, and I imagine she will want to have it retrofit so it will be wheelchair accessible. Then I pull back, my world still in the past.

Renata shares the odd and awkward comments people make to her. We exchange the odd and the awkward.

February. Renata seems more relaxed. She tells me that her sister's most appreciated gifts to her were her open-mindedness and acceptance of others, and that perhaps in leaving, Alessandra bestowed on her some of her spirited energy, because these days, her determination has renewed. "I now feel more forthright," she says. "Alessandra's compassion makes me proud of her. She had more determination than anyone I know. She quit smoking after many years. I'm tearing up as I tell you that I want to focus on my health."

March. She watches true crime shows. I watch several with her, some are cases of rape, many show the murder of a young woman, solving the mystery of how she was killed and by whom. Each episode contains interviews with the woman's parents and siblings, during which they are asked about the murdered woman's interests and their pain at her loss. There is a visit to her grave site with the family members.

April. Renata hasn't bought any clothes since her sister died. She's lost the urge for retail therapy, she tells me. But she undertakes a plan to hold a fashion show in honour of her sister's fearlessness. City Sisters is dedicated to Alessandra and is grandly successful.

Connecting with most people still challenges me. I'm changing, no longer the person I was, and unsure who I'm becoming. Sometimes this seems like a good thing. But it's tricky. Have I changed so much that Alessandra wouldn't recognize me?

My mind loops the thought that her cardiac problem was largely ignored.

We hear people say it's the worst thing that can happen to a parent; children should bury their parents; this is a reversal of how life should be. But it does happen. Sometimes our children die before we do. Six months after this happened to me, I think, no, there are worse things, and there are better things. There are no absolutes when it comes to grief.

# Unknowns

Were her nurses concerned about her level of medications?

Did they suspect she would die?

Why wasn't her cardiac issue taken seriously?

Was she considered expendable?

Did anyone feel guilty?

Did *my own depression* hold me back from fighting harder?

Did I know I had become a shell of a person?

I overhear someone I've known for many years say to someone else that I have one daughter, Renata. How did Alessandra get erased so easily?

Nervously I ring the doorbell of the host's home when after four months I return to my book club. Part way through the evening my body feels sunburnt.

A friend invites me for a long weekend in Prince Edward County. We visit cheese factories, wineries, and artists' studios. We eat gloriously and drink recklessly. And at last, I sleep well.

I no longer need to keep my phone beside my bed.

# Home

## July, away

I bring some of Alessandra's ashes to the ocean's edge on the Bonavista Peninsula in Newfoundland, where I stay for a month. They briefly colour the water as tiny wavelets trickle towards them, then lightly twirl and dance. I wave to Alessandra as the ocean takes her. *You belong here. Your life back to the sea where all our amoebic ancestors rock in the wind and waves.* Waving to her seems right. Until my waving hand holds my head.

Later that day, butterflies appear, surrounding me as I hike along Skerwink Trail. Butterflies are said to tell us that a loved one is fine. I disregard my skepticism. Alessandra walks with me, tight by my side. My mum, too, walks with us, and as I follow the trail, I understand why people say they want to join someone who has died.

# Home

## October


Thanksgiving. Finally, I go to the basement to empty the bags of Alessandra's clothes. But they aren't there. Renata has done this for me, without saying so. Such kindness, such strength. Our family of two.


My birthday without Alessandra, who would have bought me a present weeks before, and been excited to tell me what it was, to give it to me before my birthday. *Here, Mum, I just can't wait for you to open it.* We three would have gone to a restaurant for dinner.

Renata and I bravely do go to a restaurant. On the way, we come across a bird dying on the road, then find the restaurant we've chosen closed. As we enter another restaurant, my memory flashes back to a lunch that Alessandra and I once had there. By chance, our server brings us to the same table.

Later that evening, we watch a television show in which a woman reacts to hearing that her son has died. Distraught, she falls to the floor, breaking her necklace, beads falling across the carpet.

The following day, I am as unstrung as those beads.

November. Approaching the first anniversary, I'm numb to all feeling. My brain moves affect into a place hard to reach. In the early afternoon of the anniversary, it snows. My friend Carolyn and I go to high tea, which seems ironic, yet oddly appropriate. She relates how she once successfully convinced Alessandra not to buy an Irish friendship ring that she had wanted. I tell her I found a friendship ring among Alessandra's items. I lift my right hand showing it to her. We laugh.

Later that day, as Renata and I place some of Alessandra's ashes in a stream, leaning over a walking bridge, one of Renata's gloves drops into the water and is pulled by the flow. Racing over the rocks, she retrieves it before it streams by her.

"Just like Alessandra," she says.

# Home

## Year down

Narratives of experiences bracketing a year. The Year of... . . . reading a book a day, or a book from every country. The year of eating local, of yes, practiculture, of buying only second-hand objects, of not spending money. All premised on the idea that in a year's time, we can achieve a transformation.

Stories of grief, too, often follow the first year following a death. The stories end with a catharsis. The writer steps out of an emotional gutter. The shell of grief is broken and the narrator moves on, full of recommendations for others. A happy change of house or city, a new partner to embrace, a daring trip around the world. The sadness resolved.

So it is that at the end of my own year of grief, I somehow expect a release of pain. I want my step to lighten, my concentration to improve. I want unbridled energy. But there is no anniversarial effect, no sense that it is over and I can move on. Grief still clutches me, sideswipes me as I lean into it. It has become my constant. There's more of this to come; my 'year of' will be longer than 365 days.

# Propeller Dance

The Propeller Dance performance following Alessandra's death is dedicated to her. Sitting in my reserved seat, how I wish she were on stage. As I leave, an effervescent volunteer approaches to ask if I represent one of the supporting foundations.

I tell her that I'm Alesssandra's mother.

As a big smile crosses her face, she says, "She performed so well tonight."

I say nothing.

Walking outside, the moon is pencil thin, close to the ground, the sky streaking pink and black, calming.

The work I need to do now is to face my grief with more sedulousness. I feel as though I am cutting myself open as I peel back the skin from my skull to look at my altered thinking, my unhinged mind, my disabled memory. I prod my heart. I see as distractions the effort to undertake easy chatter, to be in groups, to pretend I'm fine so that no one need worry about me. I examine my feelings, sparing myself nothing. I can't afford to be vague, sloppy with grief. To hold myself together, I need dagger-like clarity.

# Home

## Almost a year and over

For close to a year, my spiritual practice doesn't serve me, or perhaps I don't let it serve me. Nevertheless, after eleven months I tentatively walk back into my spiritual life. I sit in the back row in a large room in my spiritual centre. A friend comes and sits beside me. Such kindness.

Slowly over the next year, in small steps, I reconnect more and more with my spiritual self, but with a new approach—tougher, keener, more integrated with myself. I read philosophical underpinnings to find a re-entry to my spiritual practice and discover a way back to that part of my life. I return to the questions which led me there in my early twenties—why we live, the before and the after. Now I ponder them with more urgency. Plumbing my interior life, I begin to shed numbness, my frozen state of sorrow.

I am thawing, even that pain impermanent, like all else in this connected world. All ephemeral.

# Coroner's report

After thirteen months, the post-mortem results arrive. Age, weight, height, place of residence. Histological analysis, normal; toxicology, normal. The scars on her body counted; her face peeled back; her blood sucked out; her heart taken out and weighed, a bit bigger than expected, but not abnormal. I also note this.

The report includes mistaken social information.

"We can't just remove something because someone asks us."

I tell him that so many assumptions had been made about her that I don't want that to be continued after her death. When my member of parliament intervenes, I receive a revised report.

No cause of death found.

What to say how my daughter died?

# Home

## Two years

It takes me this long before I think about what happened after Renata and I left the ward following Alessandra's death. How did her body get moved down the hall, past patients, to the hospital morgue? Then outside to a vehicle for transportation to a crematorium? Then into the crematorium?

I'm still recovering from her death and my body is still recovering from the crises, the traumas, the relentlessness of it all. Her suffering non-stop. Still in a state of waiting, waiting for something terrible to happen, and my anger, two years later. Knowing I must keep it reined in.

Each morning still I hold on. At times as I leave my home I wonder— am I stepping out of privacy, shame, shifting fear? There are small turning points, hints that I might edge forward.

One in particular. On the second anniversary of Alessandra's death I wake up with an impression that I might resolve my troubled sleeping, find, even do something interesting, live as someone in the middle of life, plan, be granted energy, perhaps become unstuck.

A sudden realization swirls up and I'm surprised that I had kept it suppressed until now. I couldn't have kept on. At some point and in some way, my body would have pinned me to a wall and kept me there—a heart attack, an accident from exhaustion, a thick depression. Did the timing of her death save me?

On the second anniversary of her death I write letters to her, from her, and from her sister.

*Dear Alessandra,*

*No more firsts. I've walked through each one. This anniversary even*
*more difficult than the first.*

*I'm sorry I didn't know how close you were to death, but were you?*

*My determination, the best home for you, never came*

*Your life's colours so bright, you changed mine to know the world bigger*

*And now your absence is further changing my life*

*more compassionate, stronger, but the empty space at the table, the not there*
*at each celebration*

*I never got to say goodbye  for the better*

*I say your name, fight against fading of memories*

*The ache not letting up even as time rushes farther away.*


*Dear mum,*

*I was the first to guide for you the way of mental illness, attempts of suicide,*
*paraplegia*

*all firsts. Your first child to die*

*Talk about me*

*Have a coffee for me, don't let new friends not know me,*

*I said I couldn't live if you died first. It would be too hard for me*

*I quit smoking months before I died, to be healthy*

*My strength to quit. I had no plan to leave life so soon*

*Sing my favourite song today LOUD What a Wonderful World*

*Dance a little, like we did, carefree and with love*

*Dear Alessandra,*

*Faithful in your protection, in your admiration of me*

*We kept the course of sisters*

*Who know, who watch each other*

*I shifted to protecting you too*

*Remembering, learning from you to be determined, daring*

*grateful*

*Always*

# Home

## Still

Three years later. I avoid sad movies, details of appalling world news, and I become a reader of obituaries—each one, someone's life summed. Each day the newspaper tells me of people leaving, leaving others to mourn. I focus on obituaries of young people, querying cause of death.

I want to talk with Alessandra, sing with her, pass morning strawberries and croissants across the kitchen table. Fill our coffee cups, lean toward her. And sometimes disagree. Challenge. Argue. Then lean toward each other again. More coffee?

But if not how it was, then how?

*Excruciating bed sore infections until gangrenous, making a route through her body?*

*Loss of eyesight, blind by diabetes?*

*Loss of leg, same cause?*

*Suicide by crash between car and wheelchair?*

I'll leave it there. Still, I am not resigned.

# Home

## Another year

A panic attack hits me two days before Alessandra's birthday, four years after her death, but no one will want to know. *Pathetic, she can't get over it. What's wrong with her?*

April. Waking up I realize that I'm forgetting how Alessandra looked and spoke, that I don't think about her as often as I once did. I have to be strict with myself, I have to stop living inside my own shadow. Anger fuels me. I want to get my life going, put newness in place, a new time.

April, one week later. A huge boulder lodges inside me. I have to heave it up and over a high cliff to get rid of it. Waves of anger overtake me, and I feel the need to be alone, to hide myself like a troglodyte.

Yet I host a dinner for eight people.

Progress? Success?

As an antidote to loss I check out dog rescue sites. I haven't had a dog for five years. I have ached for one, but I haven't been able to take the next step.

Until one evening. It's 7:00 p.m., and I notice a dog on the Humane Society's website. I hurry to the building an hour before it closes to meet the dog. He walks deliberately towards me, looks me directly in the eyes and takes my heart. He and I leave the building, me sneaking hope into my life. Maybe, just maybe, I will start to lean into life.

Settling in, he engages with the happy side of life and I snuggle with him, call him sweet names, whisper in his ear. Gosh, he is awfully cute. But what name?

Bobby. Benjy. Bennie. Bucky. Sparky. Buffy. Billy. Sweetie. Sammy. Alfie. Bertie. Bunny. Buzz. Snowy. Danny. Jeff. Serge. Moonbeam. Sunshine—Sunny for short. Sunbeam. Sunny for short. He keeps Bobby.

# Home

## Year five

Five years, will this one bring relief? I slid into the second year. The third year, reality struck. In my fourth, I told myself that by my fifth, I would step out of the grey into more colour.

I've made it here. To what?

That summer, I distract myself. I socialize hard and often. I fix my house, put in new floors upstairs and in the front hallway, paint the living room a new colour, buy a dining room table and chairs. I eat chocolate and sweets. Feel jittery and gain weight.

When my bereaved families group gets together in late August, somehow, we all forget. For almost four years, ten parents whose children have died, have met for potluck dinners, BBQ's, wine and cheese evenings every three months or so. Each time, we've talked about travel, sports, politics and work, but mostly we've talked about our kids. But this time we forget.

Small lights flicker, cicadas trill, a warm breeze stirs the flowers, big as pink plates, in a magazine-perfect garden. We eat, drink wine. It isn't until near the end of the evening when one woman says, "I feel like my daughter is here with us."

Looking toward the woman across the dim light, a few of us nod in her direction. Our voices now in the near dark, faces just barely outlined. Our talk moves back to autumn travel plans, rose gardens.

I arrive home late, relaxed. Walking through my door, an odd feeling of forgetting something catches me. Did I leave something behind? What have I forgotten? As I place my keys in the dining room on a side table close to a picture of Alessandra, she seems to look at me as if to say, *Me!*

*You forgot me and the others at the potluck. We were all there, waiting, wishing for you to mention our names.*

Then I remember. Something else, too. For the first time at our get togethers, no one said, hey, next time, my place, October?


These are the questions I still sometimes stumble over. *How many children do you have? How did your daughter die? Are you over it?* When I answer, my voice doesn't sound natural to me, although I've got better at replying, or perhaps it's that I've had more practice. Perhaps it's just that a bit more colour has returned to my world.

And why have I been hiding myself? Like an anchorite, I've walled myself off from most others. Time to break down the wall, connect.

I speak out to Barb, to Jane, to Ingrid. Each time I say that Alessandra harmed herself at nine and wanted to die at twelve and I speak out about how, following a call from a hospital to come immediately, I raced at midnight to the wrong hospital. And each time in response they open up in extraordinary ways, each conversation informing me how important it is to talk like this. I resolve not to hide myself. This is who I am.

At the same time, my mind fastens to

Her bed sores. Why was she left for hours at times in excruciating pain?

A child psychiatrist, discovered to have engaged in sexual misconduct against a patient during the same period of time my daughter was his patient

My inability to relax

The antidepressants I tried, none helpful.

Yet

Grief now comes less jarringly, at times even gently. With less exhaustion, improved cognition, I walk down the street and marvel at the setting sun in a warm kaleidoscope sky. Tiger lilies bounce at the edge of the sidewalk, and my dog stops to smell a lavender plant. I see colour all around me.

What we know and don't know, until the knowing becomes safe. Only now do I unbury a close-to-the-bone self-censorship. What I had, what I needed, was the mental health system, and its hold on me, my need for it, disallowed awareness. And those who worked within that system, my need for them.

It takes this long to consider.

The emergency psychiatrist who sent Alessandra home although she was in distress and suicidal – did he know she returned the following day?

The emergency psychiatrist who sent Alessandra home the following day although she was still in distress and suicidal – did he know that when she arrived home she jumped from her balcony?


How to define life? Is life good, is life hard, is it a mystery, a discovery, a heartache? Maybe it's unknowable, a treasure, a number of heart beats. A measure of hours, days, years, numbers, the tally of it all. Who's to say? Time spent, given away, going away, just is. A rock and a hard place, up to you.


I found myself lost, stuck in a large deciduous forest. Although crowds of people were hiking along twisting paths, no one explained to me how to find my way out. After searching for a long time, I finally arrived at the edge of the forest, and I said, maybe even out loud, *I'm finally out of the woods.* In my dream the following night, I was swimming in the deep end of a crammed swimming pool and unable to get past all the swimmers to make it to the edge of the pool and climb out. When at last I reached there, I heard myself say, *I'm out of the deep end.*

# Advice to me

*Stand firm.*

*Grief takes perhaps forever.*

*Ignore what you imagine others think of you.*

*Alessandra, you loved kindness, and I loved when others were kind to you. In turn, you were often spectacularly kind to others. People say I did a lot for you, but we were in it together and you did much for me. Thank you.*

I remember you singing *What a Wonderful World*.

You saw trees and flowers and birds. You watched the seasons change. You sang that the world is wonderful. That's what you thought. Like Louis Armstrong, Satchmo, with his fulsome trumpet playing style, who changed the way music was played and heard.

This is it. Done.

# Acknowledgments

An awesome thank you to my stellar editor, Susan Olding, to whom I am immensely indebted. I am filled with gratitude for her thoughtful and thorough editing.

Many thanks to my excellent publisher, Andrea O'Reilly of Demeter Press, for her belief in this project. Without her wonderful support, this book would not have been possible.

A heartfelt thank you to Diana Smith for her kindness and generosity. Her beautiful gift to me of her encaustic painting depicting a São Paulo favela became the cover of this book.

From the bottom of my heart, I appreciate Alessandra's friends and mine, who stood by us and with us.

For her brilliance and unfathomable wisdom, I thank my sister, Arleen. Her encouragement to me during the writing of this book means more to me than I can adequately express.

And finally, immense thanks, love, warmth, and appreciation to my daughter, Renata, who had tremendous faith in my writing of this book about our family.

# Author's Note

This book is based on my best recollections and everything I've written is as true as I remember. As meanings and inferences of words can transform over time, should any words or expressions offend a reader, I offer my apologies. I trust that this book will be a warm resource for those whose lives have been touched by troubling situations, particularly mental illness and grief. We all need an end to the stigma of mental illness.

# References

Page 19. Bruce, J., et al. "Early Adverse Care, Stress Neurobiology, and Prevention Science: Lessons Learned." *Prevention Science*, vol. 14, no. 3, 2013, pp. 247-56.

Page 24. "Project Ice Storm." *McGill*, www.mcgill.ca/projetverglas/icestorm. Accessed 3 Jan. 2019.

Page 26. University of Zurich. "Too Much Stress for the Mother Affects the Baby through Amniotic Fluid." *Science Daily*, 17 May 2017, www.sciencedaily.com/releases/2017/05/1705.

Page 28. CDC. "Adverse Childhood Experiences (ACEs) VitalSigns." *CDC*, www.cdc.gov/vitalsigns/aces/index.html. Accessed 2 Feb. 2018.

Page 30. This quote by Thales of Miletus was cited in Maria Popova, "How to be a Good Creature," https://www.brainpickings.org/2018 /10/31/ how-to-be-a-good-creature-sy-montgomery. Accessed 16 Nov. 2018.

Page 30. "The Creation of the First Greek Gods," https://www.greek-gods.info/theogony/chaos. Accessed 14 Sept. 2018.

Page 33. "Indra's Net." *Dharmapedia*, en.dharmapedia.net/wiki/Indra%27s_net. Accessed 7 Nov. 2018.

Page 42. PsychCentral, "Childhood Abuse, Complex Trauma and Epigenetics." *Psych Central*, psychcentral.com/lib/childhood-abuse-complex-trauma-and-epigenetics. Accessed 8 Dec. 2018.

Page 42. Wolff, Megan, J., "Fact Sheet: The Trauma of Childhood Separation." *Psych History*, psych-history.weill.cornell.edu/pdf/ Trauma_of_Separation.pdf. Accessed 18 Nov. 2020.

Page 43. Cleveland Clinic. "Childhood Trauma's Lasting Effects on Mental and Physical Health." *Cleveland Clinic*, health.cleveland clinic. org/childhood-traumas-lasting-effects-on-mental-and-physical-health/. Accessed 25 May 2020.

Page 50. Margaritoff, Marco. "More U.S. Veterans Have Committed Suicide In The Last Decade Than Died In The Vietnam War." *All That Is Interesting, allthatsinteresting.com/veteran-suicide.* Accessed 2 June 2020.

Page 56. Medical News Today. "What Are the Effects of Solitary Confinement on Health?" *Medical News Today,* www.medical newstoday.com/articles/solitary-confinement-effects. Accessed 11 Nov. 2020.

Page 56. Renzetti, Elizabeth. "In Solitary, There's No End and No Beginning." *The Globe and Mail,* 8 Dec. 2014, www.theglobeandmail.com/opinion/in-solitary-theres-no-end-and-no-beginning/article21976848/. Accessed 8 Dec. 2018.

Page 57. From time to time, there are news reports of the situation of mentally ill persons in solitary confinement.

Page 60. Bailey, Regina. "Spinal Cord Function and Anatomy." *Thought Co,* 14 Dec. 2018, www.thoughtco.com/the-spinal-cord-373189. Accessed 14 Dec. 2019.

Page 71. Rodrigue, Samantha. "Insights on Canadian Society: Hidden Homelessness in Canada." *Statistics Canada,* 2016, www150.statcan.gc.ca/n1/pub/75-006-x/2016001/article/14678-eng.htm. Accessed 25 July 2018.

Page 76. Kane, Suzanne. "Long-Term Effects of Chronic Stress on Body and Mind." *Psych Central,* 2016, psychcentral.com/lib/long-term-effects-of-chronic-stress-on-body-and-mind#4. Accessed 14 June 2020.

Page 78. Electric wheelchairs have a notorious reputation for breaking down. Their motors are especially fickle in winter weather.

Page 82. News reports such as this are occasionally reported.

Page 84. Sherrie Bourg Carter. "The Tell Tale Signs of Burnout ... Do You Have Them?" *Psychology Today,* 2013, www.psychologytoday.com/us/blog/high-octane-women/201311/the-tell-tale-signs-burnout-do-you-have-them. Accessed 8 Dec. 2019.

Page 85. Lewis, Feylyn. "Ambiguous Loss: When the Loss Doesn't End." *Project We Forget,* projectweforgot.com/your-aid/wellbeing/ambiguous-loss-when-the-loss-doesnt-end/. Accessed 7 Nov. 2019.

Page 89. CBC News. "Hearing Voices Workshop Gives Insight into Schizophrenia." *CBC*, 11 Mar. 2014, www.cbc.ca/news/canada/manitoba/hearing-voices-workshop-gives-insight-into-schizo phrenia. Accessed 14 Sept. 2019.

Page 98. "Secondary Traumatic Stress. What is Secondary Traumatic Stress?" U.S. Department of Health & Human Services, Administration for Children & Families, www.acf.hhs.gov/trauma-toolkit/secondary-traumatic-stress, accessed 5 April 2019.

Page 103. This is one case among a variety of cases in the news of police treatment of people with mental illness.

Page 104. Hitomaro, Kakinomoto no. "On the Sea of the Heavens." *All Poetry*, allpoetry.com/On-the-sea-of-the-heavens. Accessed 25 July 2018.

Page 104. Daishonin, Nichiren. *The Writings of Nichiren Daishonin*. Soka Gakkai, 1999.

Page 112. "Kisa Gotami and the Mustard Seed." *Buddhist Stories*, 2012, buddhiststories.wordpress.com/2012/11/03/kisa-gotami-and-the-mustard-seed. Accessed 2 June 2020.

Page 130. Harvard Women's Health Watch. "Takotsubo Cardio-myopathy (Broken-Heart Syndrome)." *Harvard Health*, www.health.harvard.edu/heart-health/takotsubo-cardiomyopathy-broken-heart-syndrome. Accessed 6 Oct. 2019.

Deepest appreciation to
Demeter's monthly Donors

**DEMETER**

**Daughters**
Rebecca Bromwich
Summer Cunningham
Tatjana Takseva
Debbie Byrd
Fiona Green
Tanya Cassidy
Vicki Noble
Bridget Boland
Naomi McPherson
Myrel Chernick

**Sisters**
Kirsten Goa
Amber Kinser
Nicole Willey
Christine Peets